Beautifully Scripted

Beautifully Scripted

Living Out Singleness in a Way that Honors Christ

Lauren McCoy

Singled Out
FOR HIM

Beautifully Scripted: Living Out Singleness in a Way that Honors Christ

ISBN-13: 978-0-578-70476-0

To all the women in this season of singleness:
You are beautiful, you are seen, and you are loved by our God.

To the Singled Out for Him community:
Thank you for walking this singleness journey with me.

Table of Contents

PROLOGUE

ACT I: The Leading Actress

ACT II: The Supporting Actors

ACT III: The Author

CREDITS

PROLOGUE

Growing up, I felt like I was getting my life cues from a script — a script that helped me ad lib impromptu moments. I always knew what my life would look like — what role my character would play. Everyone around me whispered the lines for the next scene, like a *spoiler alert* that I loved knowing. My script read smoothly and predictably. I loved acting out each scene with ease and confidence.

After high school, I *knew* the college scene was next. The whispers told me, "Oh, you'll find someone for sure!" So I headed off to college intending to become a teacher. In the back of my mind, I knew that I would meet someone, just as my character was "supposed to do." I would probably never have to actually teach because I would take care of my husband, host dinner parties, have a family, etc. Does this sound familiar? Maybe you wanted your script to read similarly.

The problem was that I didn't meet a man in college that I was interested in marrying. So I graduated with no idea what my character was to do next. It was as if I were standing on stage, delivering a beautiful monologue, at the end of which another actor was supposed to enter stage left. After several moments of awkward silence, I improvised a few lines. In my mind, I was giving the actor enough time to finish whatever he was doing and make it out to finish the scene. As the minutes ticked by, it became obvious that he was not coming. The lights bore down on me. The audience started to murmur, "What's wrong? Isn't something supposed to happen?" Silence. Slowly, I realized someone had whispered the wrong lines to me. In fact, it wasn't even my script. I was in the wrong scene.

It took years to realize that my script, though different from what I imagined, was good. I had a good part to play. The longer I listened to the true Script Writer for my lines and for direction, the more I understood that this is a story greater than I could ever have dreamed.

Although singleness may not be the role you wanted, the Author of your script chose this part for you, and it is *Beautifully Scripted*. It does not look like anyone else's. It is handwritten by God: the Creator of the world, the One Who spoke light, animals, plants, and all things into existence. He spoke, and it happened. This same God knew what purpose He had for you before you were conceived in your mother's womb. So let's listen and follow the direction of the best Script Writer and Director as we enter this scene together. Get ready — lots of drama, romance, action, and comedy to follow.

CURTAINS RISE.

ACT I

The Leading Actress

SCENE 1

Understanding My Character

Single. It's a Facebook status and a label that can quickly become your identity if you're not careful. When you meet someone for the first time, people often ask the typical questions: "What do you do for a living? Are you married? Do you have kids?" When married people hear my response to the last two questions, the conversation can take an awkward turn. "No, I'm single." Sometimes people don't know how to react, relate, or connect to this unexpected answer. But the truth is — single or not —

there is much more to us as believers than whether we are married or have children or not because our identity is rooted in Christ and who He says we are.

Your Relationship Status Doesn't Define You

You must understand this truth. It is true now in your season of singleness and will continue to be true in all seasons of life: Your marital status does not *define* you; it only *describes* you. It describes you in the same way you would describe someone as tall, short, blonde, brunette, athletic, or artistic. It does not diminish value or determine worth. Your worth and value come from something — rather Some*one* — greater: Christ and what He did on the cross.

Sister, if you are single and in Christ, *you are whole*. When asked "Are you dating anyone?" or "Why aren't you married?" so many times it makes your head spin, you may feel as if you are lacking or missing something. But Colossians 2:10a says, "in Christ you have been brought to fullness" (NIV). When you are *in* Christ, you are whole, complete, lacking nothing. Pause and meditate on this truth. Allow the Holy Spirit to minister this truth to your heart, not just your head. Then rest confidently that with Jesus you are full and complete.

My Identity

So if Christ defines me, then what does He say? Oh, girl. It is beyond comprehension. If we are in Christ, then we can confidently read these truths over ourselves:

I am a friend of Jesus. "I have called you friends" (John 15:15 HCSB).

I am a child of God. "Yet to all who did receive him, to those who believed in his name, he gave the right to become children of God" (John 1:12 NIV). God is delighted to call me His daughter. He planned for it to happen according to His perfect will: "He predestined us for adoption to sonship through Jesus Christ, in accordance with his pleasure and will" (Ephesians 1:5 NIV). "See what great love the Father has lavished on us, that we should be called children of God! And that is what we are!" (1 John 3:1a NIV).

I am an heir. "And if children, then heirs — heirs of God and fellow heirs with Christ, provided we suffer with him in order that we may also be glorified with him" (Romans 8:17 ESV). I have an inheritance.

I am accepted. "Accept one another, then, just as Christ has accepted you, in order to bring praise to God" (Romans 15:7 NIV). When others do not accept me or think less of me because of my singleness, I can rest in the fact that God accepts me.

I am chosen as God's special possession. "But you are a chosen people, a royal priesthood, a holy nation, God's special possession, that you may declare the praises of him who called you out of darkness into his wonderful light" (1 Peter 2:9 NIV). I am His. His purpose for me is to declare His praises.

I am set apart. "Before I formed you in the womb I knew you, before you were born I set you apart" (Jeremiah 1:5a NIV). Before I was even conceived, God knew me and determined that He wanted me.

I am being made new. "Therefore, if anyone is in Christ, he is a new creation; old things have passed away; behold all things have become new" (2 Corinthians 5:17 NKJV). "I am sure of this, that He who started a good work in you will carry it on to completion until the day of Jesus Christ" (Philippians 1:6 HCSB). My life isn't boring. I'm a new creation, and God is not finished with me.

I am beautifully created by God — and He did a good job at it. "I will praise you, for I am fearfully and wonderfully made; marvelous are your works, and that my soul knows very well" (Psalm 139:14 NKJV). The psalmist praises God for how awesomely He made him. I can be confident in the beauty that God has created in me — inwardly and outwardly. "For we are God's handiwork, created in Christ Jesus to do good works, which God prepared in advance for us to do" (Ephesians 2:10 NIV). God, the Artist Who paints the sunsets, molded me into a unique masterpiece. He thought of me and wanted me to be part of His plan in doing good works for His glory. "You are altogether beautiful, my darling; there is no flaw in you" (Song of Solomon 4:7 NIV). Just as Solomon woos his lover in Song of Solomon, Christ woos me by declaring my beauty.

I am bought with a price. "You were bought at a price. Therefore honor God with your bodies" (1 Corinthians 6:20 NIV). I can honor God through remaining pure sexually and mentally with my thoughts.

I am worthy. "She is worth far more than rubies" (Proverbs 31:10 NIV). God gives me value and worth far above earthly riches.

I am the Bride of Christ. "For your Maker is your husband, the LORD of hosts is his name; and the Holy One of Israel is your Redeemer, the God of the whole earth he is called" (Isaiah 54:5 ESV). Whether or not I will be a bride here on earth, I am the heavenly Bride of Christ, awaiting the marriage supper of the Lamb. My covenant with the Bridegroom is eternal and can never be broken. "For I am jealous for you with the jealousy of God himself. I promised you as a pure bride to one husband—Christ" (2 Corinthians 11:2 NLT).

Which truths spoke the most to you? Write them out on an index card. Where and when are you most often tempted to believe lies? Is it at work when all of your coworkers are talking about how you need to get married? In the car during a lonely drive home? In your bathroom while you're getting ready in the morning? In your pantry where you keep the dark chocolate that seems to want to comfort you (this is definitely me)? Put your index cards where you need the reminder (maybe make a couple of copies). We have to remind ourselves that Jesus is our Comforter — not things or people — and that He, thankfully, determines our identity.

I love the faith of Mary, an engaged young woman, who just received word of the scary yet beautiful plans God had for her. "She who has believed is blessed because what was spoken to her by the Lord will be fulfilled!" (Luke 1:45 HCSB). God called her blessed because she believed what God said. She took Him at His Word. God says these things about you. Will you believe it? Will you silence the lies of the world and the screams of your insecurities and believe the truth? Purpose in your heart that you will believe. Say it out loud over and over until it becomes the natural response of your heart.

While it is important to know who *we* are, we truly need to focus more on Who *He* is. Fears and insecurities are cast out by the knowledge of the great I AM. In *Women of the Word*, Jen Wilkin says, "The Bible does tell us who we are and what we should do, but it does so through the lens of who God is. The knowledge of God and the knowledge of self always go hand in hand. In fact, there can be no true knowledge of self apart from the knowledge of God. He is the only reference point that is reliable."[1] Start knowing God by turning the pages of Scripture.

Singleness Does Not Mean . . .
I Am Lonely

A few months ago, I was babysitting two sweet little girls. Over pizza and a bowl of ice cream, the questions started coming.

> Girls: "How many kids do you have?"
> Me: "I don't have any."
> Girls: "Do you have a husband?"
> Me: "Nope."
> Girls: "You're not married! Do you have a boyfriend?"
> Me: "No."

I'm starting to squirm a little bit. *Why am I letting these questions from five- and nine-year-olds bother me?* I find myself not measuring up — even in their eyes. I find myself not fitting into their idea of where I should be because, after all, I am an adult. And with being an adult comes a spouse and children. Right?

They asked a few more questions: "Do you live alone? Do you have friends?" Finally, the conversation ended. We moved on to American Girl dolls and Bitty Babies. My mind, however, lingered on our exchange.

Later that night, the parents came home as I was putting the girls to bed. The mom came into the room with the littlest girl, and we all said our goodnights. Right before the mom shut the door, the little girl yelled out with a hint of panic in her voice, "Mom! Miss Lauren is ALL ALONE."

Alone. The word even sounds cold. Even this five-year-old girl realized the scariness of feeling lonely. I think we would all acknowledge that we fear this feeling. It's not that we aren't comfortable being alone at times, but it's different when you start to feel as if your life is being defined as solitary, lonely, desolate.

The truth is, we can be lonely in any season of life. We can be lonely in singleness. We can be lonely in dating. We can be lonely in marriage. We can be lonely in a room full of people.

So if your relationship status doesn't fix loneliness and being around people doesn't help, what does?

Wisdom.

Wisdom is what allows you to see the truth in your circumstances. And where is this wisdom found? In the Bible. Proverbs 4:6 commands, "Do not forsake [wisdom], and she will keep you; love her, and she will guard you" (ESV). Interestingly, I was reading an article on the correlation between wisdom and loneliness and was amazed at how biblical the research was despite the secular source.

The researchers found that people who did not feel lonely often had high levels of wisdom. They measured "the six components of wisdom in each participant: general knowledge of life; emotion management; empathy, compassion, altruism and a sense of fairness; insight; acceptance of divergent values; and decisiveness."[2] People who were wise and mature in these specific areas were less lonely than their peers who were found to be more immature in these components.

Who gives wisdom in all areas of life? God. James 1:5 tells us, "Now if any of you lacks wisdom, he should ask God — who gives to all generously and ungrudgingly — and it will be given to him" (CSB). You can be wise, and you don't have to be lonely.

As I drove home from babysitting that rainy Friday night, I thanked God that while the world or well-meaning children might look sadly at my circumstance — no husband, no kids, no boyfriend, I can rest confidently in the fact that I am not alone. God's Word tells me He will never leave me nor forsake me. I find comfort in that wisdom.

I Am "Less Than"

In a world of marriage and relationships, being single can leave you feeling "less than." I hear the lies whispering that because no one has chosen me as a spouse, I am not good enough or pretty enough; I am "less than" my married sisters-in-Christ. It seems that I am not really a catch because if I were — where are all the men who are supposed to be lining up at my door?

Despite my feelings and destructive whisperings from the enemy, I must remember that I am, in fact, chosen. If I am chosen by a holy and perfect God (remember our identity statements), then that leaves no room for feeling "less than." Don't allow your relationship status or feelings to dictate your worth. God calls you worthy.

I Must Prove Myself

Sometimes I feel awkward being single. I feel as if I have to prove that I am enough — just me, without a spouse — so I work to prove myself. I hold my head up high, show no sign of struggle or weakness. I do. I serve. I busy myself.

I feel good about myself when I'm busy. Busyness is a badge to prove that I am good and that I lack nothing. When empty places appear in my life, I fill them with busyness — even good busyness like serving or loving others; but God never asks me to prove myself.

Instead, Jesus invites me to rest. I can be enough in my singleness because His work on the cross was enough. No accomplishments or lack of accomplishments can prove my completeness. Jesus brings completeness into my life. My pastor, Brady Cooper, once said, "My identity is not in the sweat of my brow but in the blood of the cross." I need that truth. I cannot earn God's love. I cannot work myself to more grace. I do not need to prove my worth by what I do. God loves me because He is love. God gives me grace because He is gracious. I am worthy because He calls me worthy.

You are loved, Sister. You are worthy. You are enough in Him. Rest in the finished work of Christ. You have nothing to prove.

Live with Purpose

While we have nothing to prove, we have purpose to our lives, and we are called to live *with* purpose and to live *on* purpose. It is easy to scroll our way through life, liking and lusting after Instaposts, yet walk in complacency, wishing for what we don't have and lacking intentionality.

I have been doing a lot of learning, reading, listening, and growing in this area. Writing out a purpose statement has helped me live intentionally. Because priorities change with each season, I reevaluate my purpose statement at the beginning of each year and sometimes even throughout the year. Every New Year, I spend time reflecting on the gifts God has given me, areas of serving to which I feel called, and the personality I have been given. I sit down and craft a personal purpose statement for that year. When opportunities arise in my life, I hold them against my mission statement for clarity and guidance before making a decision. For the most part, if the opportunity does not line up with that statement and I don't feel the Lord leading me to commit to it, then I do not say yes. I must be intentional about how I spend my time. God has given the body of Christ a variety of talents, gifts, and passions. I believe we should live intentionally according to what has been given to us so we can faithfully live out our role. My *no* could be space for someone else's *yes*.

I start each day by claiming my purpose and asking for God to open my eyes to what He has for me. Lackadaisical days, deprived of purpose and intentionality, result in a life lived for self and devoid of potential joy. As women of God, we must purpose each day — not looking ahead and not looking behind — but looking at the day right in front of us. Today. *Carpe diem*. Seize the day. Elisabeth Elliot wisely said, "The life of faith is lived one day at a time, and it has to be lived — not always looked forward to as though the 'real' living were around the next corner. It is today for which we are responsible. God still owns tomorrow."[3] We are responsible for today — our choices, our attitudes, our interactions, our purpose. Singleness can be an easy season to waste while longing for the next season.

Living on purpose does not mean there are no mundane days. Life is made up of the mundane. It is not made up of Instastories and glorious adventures. Yes, those are fun. And God delights in sprinkling those into our day-to-day lives. However, the days, the hours, the minutes, and the seconds are made up of moments. Moments of unloading the dishwasher. Moments of getting up to go to work five or six days a week. Moments of conversations with co-workers and family members. Moments of folding clothes at the end of the day. What will you do with those moments? If I am living on purpose, I am utilizing that moment of unloading the dishwasher to sing praises to God. I am getting up and going to work with the knowledge that I am not just there to make a living; I am there to make a spiritual impact in my sphere of influence. Conversations with coworkers provide opportunities to shine God's light, show love, encourage others, and speak truth. Folding clothes results in prayer, reflection, or crying out.

I realized the importance of the mundane when I studied abroad in Spain one semester in college. I stayed with missionaries and had intentions of learning from them and seeing how they did ministry. I am such an adventurer. I love the thrill of exploring, traveling to new cities, and encountering new experiences. So my expectations were those of people being saved left and right, putting on VBS, holding Bible studies, etc. However, I found that ministry takes place in the mundane. Missionaries have to cook meals and unload the dishwasher. (What!?)

They spend time in the Word in the morning and then do chores. Sometimes it takes years of interactions with the people in the town they serve before anyone wants to have a spiritual conversation, yet they live intentionally in the mundane. Going to the grocery store is an opportunity to speak to their regular cashier and ask how they can pray for him or her. Walking around town is a time to meet and talk with their neighbors. Teaching English classes is perfect for sharing faith. Ministry involves years of hard labor and purpose, sprinkled with fruit here and there.

It was in Spain that I learned how to faithfully pray scripture and purpose over my life. The host missionary wrote a book about his prayer journey.[4] After reading it, I felt challenged to choose and pray my own life verses. I used Paul's example in Romans 1:1-6 to write my daily prayer mantra:

> I, Lauren, beloved and uniquely designed, am singled out to spread God's Good News through my gifts of teaching and encouragement. I feel called to help bring about the obedience of faith in those around me, namely people of other cultures and women in the season of singleness.

Take the time to write out your daily prayer mantra and speak it over yourself.

I, (name), (who God says you are), am singled out to (calling) through my gifts of (gifts). Specifically at this time, I feel called to (calling) among (specific people or groups of people). May I glorify You in this way.

What are your gifts? Where are you now? Ask those around you who love you. Search the Scriptures. Read the beginning of Paul's letters. You will have different purpose statements for different seasons of your life. Know your purpose in this season and start intentionally living out your identity.

SCENE 2

The Mind

Your singleness struggles start in the mind. Your mind is powerful. What we meditate on dictates how we are feeling and what we can do. The mind can be a prison or a place of liberation. Proverbs 3:5-8 commands us to "Trust in the LORD with all your heart, and do not rely on your own understanding; think about Him in all your ways, and He will guide you on the right paths. Don't consider yourself to be wise; fear the LORD and turn away from evil. This will be healing for your body and strengthening for your bones" (HCSB).

In my early 20s, I experienced a difficult time of loneliness. It was the Christmas break before I was about to graduate, and I was away from my immediate family for the holidays. I did not know my plans for after graduation, but I knew that a relationship and marriage were not in the picture. No one was on the horizon for me. My hopes, dreams, and goals since I was a little girl were not working out. After all, the script I wanted for my life read — go to college, meet the man of my dreams, graduate with a degree, get married, work my dream job for a bit, then start a family. My dream life would have closely resembled that of June Cleaver from the 1950s hit sitcom *Leave It To Beaver*. But things were not going according to plan so I started to freak out. I allowed the fear of the future to creep in. I internalized lies of "not good enough, not cared for, not loved," and I started feeling sick. Physically sick. My hair started falling out. My face broke out, and I struggled with circulation issues. I had allowed worry and distrust in God to overtake my mind, leading to physical and mental struggles. I was not happy.

God really had to do a work in my life. It didn't happen overnight. It took time. It took months of my learning to trust Him and taking Him at His Word. It took godly women speaking into my life. I had to retrain my mind to trust God with my plans. God had to penetrate my heart and thoughts with His truth. Then gratitude started to overcome ingratitude. Trust replaced distrust. Hair started to regrow. Skin began to clear. Circulation improved. The healing of the heart and mind mended what was broken.

Never underestimate the power of your mind and your meditations.

Stop Feeling Sorry for Yourself

Pity Party: Party of One. Do you ever start feeling sorry for yourself? Singleness can sometimes be one big pity party. Your mind wanders, and you start to think about how your life is miserable. You get out the decorations and start to put up the banner. "My Life Is the Worst." You blow up the balloons. "I don't understand why my life can't be *this* way. Why me?" You hang up the streamers of complaining and grumbling and throw the confetti of bitterness. Blah blah blah.

STOP. No one wants to come to your party.

In any season, not just singleness, we can start focusing too much on our problems. We think too much of ourselves and our situation and too little of other people. My grandmother Ninny used to say, "When you start feeling sorry for yourself, you need to go find something to do for someone else." When you feel the darkness of grumbling start to creep in, cancel your pity party and go do something for someone else. Write an encouraging card to someone who is hurting. Invite a friend over for coffee. Bring a meal to a new mom. You can find great joy and fun in a party of two or more.

Meditations

The pity party mentality originates from a focus on self but is also influenced by other factors, such as what we intake. We have heard it said that you become what you behold. In other words, you become and start thinking about what you set in front of you. If you find yourself organizing a pity party, ask yourself, "What do I spend my time watching? Listening to? Talking about? Looking at?" Eventually your mind is consumed with those thoughts.

Netflix Queue

Many of the movies we allow ourselves to watch will leave us entertained but with the wrong philosophies. "If you look this way, then you'll get the guy." "It feels right; therefore, it is right." "If you are true to your heart, love wins." "Do whatever makes you happy." These deceptions masquerade as truths; but when unmasked, they are not biblical. I'm not saying not to watch movies, but do not let movies be the main food source that you are consuming. Phillip Holmes says, "Although these devices and platforms aren't inherently evil or sinful, they become dangerous when we develop habits of defaulting to them *primarily* or *alone*, allowing them to become our means of escape from the complexities and inconveniences of life into the more easily controlled world of fantasy."[1] Watching too many romantic movies may only intensify your longing for love and leave you with unrealistic expectations for relationships.

What you allow your eyes to consume can bring light to your loneliness or darkness to your struggle. Matthew 6:22-23 states, "The eye is the lamp of the body. If your eye is good, your whole body will be full of light. But if your eye is bad, your whole body will be full of darkness. So if the light within you is darkness — how deep is that darkness!" (HCSB). Consider what you are letting into your soul through your eye — light or darkness.

Power in Presence

There is power in presence. What people or ideas are you allowing to have a presence in your life? Think about your struggles and think about what you are doing that could make the struggle worse. Do you struggle with body image? Following models and flipping through fitness magazines isn't going to help. Are you feeling lonely? A heavy dose of country love songs won't fix that. Up to your ears in debt? The Amazon app may need to be deleted from your phone and the fashion bloggers unfollowed.

Who you follow on Instagram and who you allow to have a presence in your life will begin to influence your thoughts and beliefs. If not aligned with God's Word, your heart will become desensitized to the truth. Be careful. In Psalm 101:3, David purposes in his heart saying, "I will not set anything worthless before my eyes. I hate the practice of transgression; it will not cling to me" (HCSB).

Meditate on Truth

The best thing to consistently fill your mind with is truth. In John 6:63, Jesus says, "The Spirit is the One who gives life. The flesh doesn't help at all. The words that I have spoken to you are spirit and are life" (HCSB). The Bible contains Words of Life. Choose to saturate yourself with the truth. Play Christian music. Have encouraging conversations with friends. Listen to a sermon. Sit down, open your Bible, pray as you go throughout the day, and allow the Spirit to speak truth into your season.

Stop Listening to Yourself

Whenever I wallow in self-pity, my mom always says, "Stop listening to yourself and start talking to yourself." Paul Tripp echoes by saying, "No one is more influential in your life than you are, because no one talks to you more than you do."[2] I think about how I feel after I spend time hanging out with certain friends. Their positivity or negativity profoundly impacts me over time. It is the same with yourself. You start listening to how you feel, and then it becomes who you are and what you do. Instead of listening to your emotions, talk to your emotions. *No, I will not feel sorry for myself. I am a child of God. I am holy, set-apart, called by God. Therefore, despite the difficulties in my life, I will choose to be joyful.*

Give Thanks

Singleness has many different seasons:

Whether you are not dating and wish you had a boyfriend . . .
Whether you are dating and wish you were engaged . . .
Whether you are engaged and wish you were married . . .
Whether you are divorced and wish you were reunited . . .
Whether you are a single mom and wish you had a husband . . .
Whether you are widowed and miss the love of your life . . .

Embrace the season you are in. Give thanks. Allow your heart to be content with where God has you now, today. Fill your mind with truth from a God Who cares. This is reason to celebrate!

SCENE 3

What Did I Do Wrong?

Singleness can sometimes feel like punishment. We like to think of life as "A + B = C," or "If I obey God, do what He wants, and God is who He says He is, then I will receive what I pray for and want in life." The Christian life is not a formula, and the Prosperity Gospel[1] is not the true gospel. But when the desires of our life are not being fulfilled, we can start to believe several lies about why we are still single.

Lies About Why You are Single

"When You are Fully Satisfied with God, He Will Bring Along the Right Person."

I have had people say something similar to this to me countless times to comfort me during times of struggling with singleness. Not only is this a lie packaged with unfounded hopes, but it is also a lie wrapped with wrong motives. It is dangerous to view *satisfaction* in God as a means of bringing along the right person, not a means of living out our intended purpose. In Psalm 62:5 David says, "For God alone, O my soul, wait in silence, for my hope is from Him" (ESV). Our soul waits for God alone. We are created to long for God. We should not long for God in order to get a man. We should be fully satisfied with God and God alone.

"When You Become the Right Person, You Will Meet the Right Person."

It is also dangerous to view *sanctification* as a means of getting a man, not a means of becoming more like Christ. The world rewards good behavior and punishes bad behavior, so we think that God operates in the same way. We think if we faithfully obey Him and become more like Him, then we will have a happy, healthy life and get what we ask for. We also think if we disobey Him or mess up, then He will punish us by withholding good from us. Our trials, difficult circumstances, and unfulfilled desires cannot be viewed through these earthly glasses. To clarify, God does reward good and punish bad, but He also sees the bigger picture and sometimes chooses to wait and reward or punish in the Age to come. We don't always get the rewards or fulfillment of promises in this life.

I am reminded of Job's friends. They ascribed Job's trials to sin and fed him lies in their explanations. In Job 15:20a, his friend reasons that "A wicked man writhes in pain all his days" (HCSB). Really? How many of you know a wicked person who, according to the world's standards, has lived a happy, wealthy life? I know quite a few.

His friend also says, "Consider: who has perished when he was innocent? Where have the honest been destroyed?" (Job 4:7 HCSB). This question posed by Job's friend is not consistent with Scripture and with our life experiences. How many of us have known people who have obeyed and served the Lord but still endured the most difficult of trials? I know I have.

One of Job's friends recommends that his trials will go away "if you redirect your heart and lift up your hands to Him in prayer — if there is iniquity in your hand, remove it" (Job 11:13-14a HCSB). Should we pray harder? Paul, a righteous servant of the Lord, prayed for his request three times, and the Lord didn't give him what he asked for (2 Corinthians 12:8). If our prayer isn't according to God's will, neither earnest pleas nor persistent requests will guarantee the answer we desire.

The reasonings of Job's friends are faulty because they are from man, not from God. This logic is similar to today's thoughts on singleness. God's truth is that our singleness is not determined by our levels of satisfaction or our pursuit of God.

"Maybe God Isn't Done with You Yet?"

God is not done with any of us yet. Paul comforts us as he comforted the Philippians in that he was "sure of this, that He who started a good work in you, will carry it on to completion until the day of Christ Jesus" (Philippians 1:6 HCSB). Married. Single. Divorced. Widowed. 20 years old. 90 years old. If you are in Christ and still breathing, He is still working. There will never be a moment of "arriving" or "completion" in our sanctification until we see Jesus face to face.

Think of how Job might have responded had he known of the conversation between God and Satan documented in the first chapter. Just like the reasons for Job's suffering were never revealed to him, we do not know why the Lord has allowed some things in our lives and has withheld others. Instead, we have to trust that He has a good purpose and a plan.

"God Has Forgotten Me."

In the Sermon on the Mount, Jesus tells His followers, "Are not five sparrows sold for two pennies? And not one of them is forgotten before God. Why, even the hairs of your head are all numbered. Fear not; you are of more value than many sparrows" (Luke 12:6-7 ESV). God cares for the birds of the air. How much more then does He care and provide for you, His daughter, the One He sent His Son to die for? Romans 8:32 says, "He who did not spare his own Son, but gave him up for us all — how will he not also, along with him, graciously give us all things?" (NIV). He knows the desires of your heart. Look for how God is providing for your longings, even if it doesn't look the way you thought it would. He has not forgotten your requests. He is always kind and giving.

Remember Truth

Singleness is not a result of your doing something wrong. It is not punishment. It is not judgment. It is not a bad thing. You did not do anything wrong to earn this season, sister. Singleness is a gift from God. It is a means for God's goodness and faithful love to chase after you. Change your perspective and see this season as a display of God's lavish love and delight. Lysa TerKeurst, in her *Trustworthy* study, wisely said,

> We have to fight the urge to expect our version of God's good timing, God's good provision, and God's good protection to match what we script for our lives. A big part of learning to rely on a trustworthy God is resetting how we define *good*. Some other words we may have to redefine are *peace* and *security* and

strength and allow God's definition to invade our reality.[2]

Remember the truth. Believe this about your satisfaction and sanctification: *When I am satisfied with God, I gain the blessings of an intimate relationship with the Savior of my soul. No man — except the God Man — can satisfy me in this way. How I am today is not how I will be tomorrow because God is continuing His work in me. Singleness is a good season in my life; it is not punishment. God has not forgotten me. I am always on His heart and mind.*

When Singleness Seems Like Suffering

Let's go back to the book of Job. This book is full of complex, wonderful truths. As I was reading the first two chapters, I was struck by what I learned about God. God is bragging on one of His children. He is showing how much He delights in the way that Job is living. When Satan comes before the Lord, God asks him, "Have you considered my servant Job? No one else on earth is like him, a man of perfect integrity, who fears God and turns away from evil" (Job 1:8 CSB). John Piper says, "It's as though a diamond thief should meet the owner at the back of a jewelry store late at night. The owner says, 'What are you doing?' And the thief answers, 'Just walking around in your store.' And then the owner says, 'Did you see our most precious diamond up there at the front?'"[3]

This made me smile. God delights so much when His children — His daughters — are living with integrity, when they fear God and not man, when they turn away from evil and pursue righteousness. This comment concerning Job provokes a dialogue between Satan and God which then leads to God allowing Satan, within His sovereign boundaries, to destroy things in Job's life. Essentially, God allows and oversees Job's suffering. This book causes a lot of people to struggle. *Wait. A good God allows suffering?* This is not an easy thought to ponder. However, with God's faithful love in mind, I can marvel at my God's delight in His children and in His confidence that Job would, although not perfectly, glorify Him in the suffering. God had a purpose in Job's trials.

Some people see singleness as suffering because it is not what they wanted for their life; they long for marriage, companionship, and children of their own. Singleness then becomes associated with God's withholding of dreams or God's judgment. This is an incorrect view of God and a misunderstanding of His goodness.

What if God has allowed singleness in our lives — just as He allowed suffering in Job's life — to reveal His glory? Or to prove that we would remain faithful to Him no matter what? What if God is bragging on His daughters — who are clothed in the righteousness of Jesus, empowered by the Holy Spirit — and saying, "Have you considered my daughter, _____? No one else on earth is like her. She is a woman of integrity, who fears God and turns away from evil. I have put her in this season of singleness because this is the best way right now for her to reveal her devotion to Me. Oh, how I delight in her!"

I love Job's responses when hardship comes. In Job 1:21 he says, "Naked I came from my mother's womb, and naked shall I return. The LORD gave, and the LORD has taken away; blessed be the name of the LORD" (ESV). The Lord gives us good things, and the Lord takes things away. His name is to be blessed! Then in Job 2:10b he asks, "Shall we receive good from God, and shall we not receive evil?" (ESV). (More on this in the "What if" section later in this book.) Are we only going to praise and serve God when He gives us what we want? How shallow, one-sided, self-glorifying is our relationship with God? May we receive the good and the hard from God with praise-filled lips. No matter what we do or do not get, or however incomprehensible our seasons of singleness, may our faith never be destroyed!

While we cannot always determine what is in the mind of the Lord, we can trust that the fulfilled dreams and the unfulfilled dreams are all from the loving and good hand of God. Job and his friends never knew about the conversation between Satan and God; God only reveals it to the reader. Finally, Job decides to put faith in the goodness of God and hope of redemption. God wanted Job to humbly surrender to His sovereignty and kindness. We, like Job, may never know why; but we must trust in the Supreme Lord of all. May our hearts echo Psalm 62:8. "Trust in Him at all times, O people; pour out your heart before Him; God is a refuge for us" (ESV).

In response to Job's questions about his pain and suffering, God revealed His character and Who He was. He never explained why; that was not His purpose. Sometimes in my singleness, I want to know, "Why me?" I question God about why He has allowed or withheld certain things in my life. I may or may not ever get answers to my questions. Just like Job, I must press into the character of God. I must focus on Who He is, not what He does or does not do in my life.

James reminds us that we "have heard of the steadfastness of Job, and you have seen the purpose of the Lord, how the Lord is compassionate and merciful" (James 5:11 ESV). We can see God's divine intentions in Job's life. We may never know His purposes in our own circumstances, but we can remain steadfast like Job and allow our eyes to see the compassion and mercy of the Lord. Job replies to the Lord, "Surely I spoke about things I did not understand, things too wonderful for me to know" (Job 42:3b HCSB). God has incomprehensible things for us — things too wonderful for us to grasp on this side of heaven.

So when singleness seems like suffering or punishment, remember these truths about life's hard seasons. Thank God for the incomprehensible things. And remain steadfast in your faith.

SCENE 4

Living the Life

Each season comes with its struggles and blessings, its pluses and minuses. When you start having the right mindset about singleness, you begin realizing one of the biggest blessings of singleness: freedom.

Now I'm not talking a Beyoncé "All the Single Ladies" lifestyle, a do-what-I-please independence, or a Shania Twain's "Man, I Feel Like a Woman" empowerment. I'm talking about having fun, traveling, building purposeful relationships, serving, deepening your intimacy with Jesus, and enjoying to the fullest the sweet gift of singleness. Singleness can be the time of your life.

Living the Life Spiritually
Free to Live Out Our Calling

While the ladies at your church, concerned about your happiness, are trying to find you a husband, Paul is urging you to remain single. He saw singleness as having the ability to focus on serving the Church rather than being distracted by the responsibilities that come with a husband and kids. He saw the blessings of not being married — the main blessing being devotion to Jesus. Paul, in his own opinion, points out that "an unmarried woman or a virgin is concerned about the things of the Lord, so that she may be holy both in body and in spirit. But a married woman is concerned about the things of the world — how she may please her husband" (1 Corinthians 7:34b HCSB). During this season of singleness, Paul challenges us to embrace the high calling of being whole-heartedly concerned about God's things. This season does not come without great purpose and responsibility.

Free to Study the Word

In order to be concerned about the things of the Lord, we must get to know Him and what He is concerned about. We must become women who know and love the Bible. Jen Wilkin says that "the heart cannot love what the mind does not know" and "to know Him is to love Him."[1] We should have the priority of sitting at Jesus' feet so that we can know Him and receive our purpose from Him. Being with Christ increases our love for Him. If you are too busy to spend time with God, then your priorities are misplaced; consider simplifying your life. Your highest priority ought to be to "set your mind and heart to seek the LORD your God" (1 Chronicles 22:19a ESV).

Study the Word. It is time that we as single women stop becoming experts on ourselves and on the lives of others and start becoming experts in God's Word. Use your time to be a student of the Bible so that you will "in your hearts honor Christ the Lord as holy, always being prepared to make a defense to anyone who asks you for a reason for the hope that is in you; yet do it with gentleness and respect" (1 Peter 3:15 ESV). Be ready to answer anyone who asks you why you are living your singleness the way you are. The world says that singleness is a time to serve self, fulfill your fantasies and desires, and do whatever you want. Naturally, people will ask, "Why are you serving at church? Why are you pursuing sexual integrity? Why aren't you doing _____? Why do you _____?" Use these questions as opportunities to gently and respectfully share the purpose and the hope that is in you during this season of singleness.

Women who know the Bible are prepared to wisely speak truth to themselves and to friends at any time and in any situation. I am reminded of what Jesus says in Matthew 13:52: "And he said to them, 'Therefore every scribe who has been trained for the kingdom of heaven is like a master of a house, who brings out of his treasure what is new and what is old'" (ESV). When you are educated and learned in God's kingdom, you are like the owner of a store who can get anything for a customer who comes in looking for what they want or need. The Spirit will bring to mind the truth that is needed for the precise moment. A wise woman also knows how to listen and when to be silent. As Proverbs 25:11 says, "A word fitly spoken is like apples of gold in a setting of silver" (ESV). God can give us the wisdom of knowing when to speak and when to refrain from speaking. We can become women of golden-apple words and settings-of-silver counsel.

What I love most about the season of singleness is that I truly have time to get to know my Jesus. While knowing my purpose, being prepared with an answer, and knowing how to advise a friend are important, nothing supersedes knowing God. Seasons of helping a husband or taking care of babies or tutoring my children may or may not come, but these are the days when I can guarantee myself time with Him. Each morning I make it a priority to have my date with Jesus. I get my coffee, my Bible, and my journal and let the Spirit move. These are the good days that I will cherish forever.

Free to Serve

You are free to serve. My time of singleness has allowed me to teach four- and five-year-old Sunday School, lead women's Bible studies, teach children's groups, play violin on the worship team, and mentor women. Galatians 5:1, 13-14 reminds us of our freedom and the way it should be used: "Christ has liberated us to be free. Stand firm then and don't submit again to a yoke of slavery . . . For you were called to be free, brothers; only don't use this freedom as an opportunity for the flesh, but serve one another through love. For the entire law is fulfilled in one statement: Love your neighbor as yourself" (HCSB). Use your freedom in Christ and your freedom in singleness as an opportunity to love other people. Use your gifts and talents — whether it's playing music, teaching, holding open the church doors, putting together the PowerPoint for worship, working in the nursery, writing encouraging cards — to serve the local church and its members.

Free to be Flexible

Another beauty of singleness is having the freedom of flexibility. When an opportunity to help others arises, you have the freedom to serve. Singleness comes with the availability to jump in at the last minute when needed.

Sometimes I can get plans and to-do lists so stuck in my head that I end up missing out on opportunities to love on others. The plans either bind me or I choose to do what I want to do. One Sunday I had big intentions to get things done after church when my eyes were opened to see the need of a sister-in-Christ. Her eyes hungered for encouragement. The Lord gently reminded me of my freedom of flexibility. So I prayed that the nagging "you have things to do" voice would leave me. I laid my agenda aside to spend the next few hours at a restaurant and a nail salon just listening.

I left our few hours together thanking the Lord that my agenda consisted of things that could wait. I did not have the responsibility of rushing off to put kids down for a nap. Instead, I had the freedom to linger over a kale and balsamic salad and to speak words of encouragement. I thanked Him that I didn't have to check plans with a husband first but could immediately say "Yes" and enjoy the hot pink nail color we chose to get.

Are a husband and kids a blessing? Yes. Do I desire a husband to ask and some kids to put down for a nap? Definitely. However, right now God has called me to this season of singleness, and I want to thank Him for the holy freedom that goes with it.

Enjoy the season God has called you to today. Don't wish it away. "Nevertheless, each person should live as a believer in whatever situation the Lord has assigned to them" (1 Corinthians 7:17a NIV). Another version says, "And don't be wishing you were someplace else or with someone else. Where you are right now is God's place for you. Live and obey and love and believe right there. God, not your marital status, defines your life" (MSG).

Our freedom is for the Lord. Christian author and pastor Sam Allberry says, "We need to remind ourselves, daily, that our singleness is not for us but for the Lord. It's not for our concerns, but his."[2] Be on the lookout for ways to be intentional about using your holy freedom and flexibility for Jesus.

Free to Build Relationships

Singleness comes with the time and flexibility to build intentional relationships — namely a deep mentor relationship and a strong mentee relationship.

Find a Paul. Paul mentored Timothy and the churches that he wrote letters to. He challenged them to "join in imitating me, brothers, and observe those who live according to the example you have in us" (Philippians 3:17 HCSB). In Titus 2, he sets a biblical model of mentorship by instructing the older women in the church to encourage the younger. I have a mentor that I meet with often who is older and wiser. I share my struggles with her, seek counsel regarding hard situations, and ask for specific prayer. I text her when overcome with temptation. I send her a message when I am discouraged. Susanne is there to offer perspective, truth from God's Word, and a good hug. Look for a lady in your church who is obedient to God and who is living a life for Jesus that you want to imitate. Ask her to go to coffee. Sit and glean wisdom from her. Ask her those hard questions. Be vulnerable with your struggles. Pray together.

Find a Timothy. When you are being poured into, you are able to pour into others. Paul finds Timothy, a young disciple of Jesus, and brings him along on his journeys. Timothy became like a son to him. Later, Paul writes him letters offering words of wisdom regarding his ministry. Like Paul, find someone who is younger, new in their faith, or struggling, and bring her alongside you in your singleness journey. Show her the contentment, joy, and peace God offers. Disciple her in reading God's Word. Be a Paul to a Timothy.

Free to Make Every Effort

People either place a heavy "do" on the Christian journey or want to run far away from it. We either tend to work to feel like we are good Christians or we neglect good works and become spiritually lazy because it is God Who does the work. But truly, the walk of faith is both — you working and God working in you. In your singleness, make the "do" a priority. Peter tells us, "For this very reason, make every effort to supplement your faith with goodness, goodness with knowledge, knowledge with self-control, self-control with endurance, endurance with godliness, godliness with brotherly affection, and brotherly affection with love. For if these qualities are yours and are increasing, they will keep you from being useless or unfruitful in the knowledge of our Lord Jesus Christ" (2 Peter 1:5-8 HCSB). We are called to make every effort to build our faith and to be more like Jesus. This is called sanctification.

Sanctification is not a means to an end. It is not to be used to manipulate God. And it is definitely not about becoming the right person for your future husband. People like to say, "If you are chasing after God, then you will one day look over and see a godly man chasing after God too." I have seen God bring two people together who weren't chasing after Him, and I have seen godly women chase after God and never have men come alongside them in their journeys. God does not operate according to a formula. Following Jesus is not "if I am like this or do this, then God will do that." Truly, sanctification is about being more like Jesus in order to glorify Him. So pursue Christ for the sake of pursuing Him and being obedient to His call. If you have ulterior motives, you will be disappointed because you will miss out on enjoying the One you are trying to be like.

Living the Life Socially

I lived the first couple of my post-college single years thinking, "When I get married, I'm going to _____ _____" and would fill in the blank with anything from traveling to taking dance lessons. Slowly, I started to realize that I could not put my life on hold. I started to ask myself, "why not now?" Marriage is not when you start life. Life is happening now. Plus, what if you never get married? Or what if you don't get married until you are 30? 40? 50? Are you going to waste those years dreaming? Start finding a way to do the things you have longed to do. There is no better time than now to do what you want to fill in the blank with.

Free to Go to Events

When I first moved to the Nashville area, I lived by myself and only knew extended family. Something I enjoyed doing in college was going to concerts and shows. The difficulty was that, though I finally had more financial freedom to go to events, I lacked a friend base with whom to attend. I would see events I wanted to go to, but I didn't have anyone to go with me.

So one day I finally just bought two tickets and prayed.

The first time I did this was to see Beauty and the Beast at the performing arts center downtown. A week before the show I still needed someone to go with. I had just started to attend a small group and hardly knew anyone, but there was a girl named Elisa who seemed fun. So I asked her to go. That night was the start of our friendship. We went to so many shows and concerts after that. It was a risk to ask because I hardly knew her, but it ended up being well worth it.

I still do this today. If there is an event coming up, I buy two tickets and pray for God to show me who to invite. Then I'll find a friend, split the costs, and enjoy a fun experience together.

Don't let singleness hold you back from enjoying events you love. Need friends? Find them. The Bible says people who show themselves friendly have friends (Proverbs 18:24 NKJV). Stop waiting to be asked, and start asking!

Free to Travel

I love traveling. It rejuvenates my spirit. I love new sights, delicious cuisine, and local coffee shops. If you love to travel, too, don't put life on hold waiting for a husband to travel with you. Now is the time to go!

I set aside money in a travel fund each month and start dreaming of where to go next. I have flown by myself to visit friends in other cities and countries — from Chicago to Utah to Spain. However, when exploring a new city, I feel much more comfortable and safe traveling with a friend, so I start asking friends to see who will be my next travel companion. I've been with both friends and family. Many memories have been made with many more to come. In my post-college single years, I have traveled with others to London, Edinburgh, Seattle, Boston, Austin, San Francisco, and Chattanooga. If you love to travel, enjoy the freedom of singleness and go! Where will you go next?

Free to Enjoy Holidays

Holidays can be so lonely and difficult to navigate as a single. There are never-ending questions from aunts, uncles, grandparents, and distant relatives. Extra grace is needed during the holiday season — grace to give yourself and grace to give others. Remember that most of these people have the purest of intentions and love you dearly. Use these opportunities to laugh and respond with grace, joy, and the light of Jesus.

Holidays are also often coupled with (pun intended) romantic traditions and longings to spend time with a special someone. There is mistletoe and hot chocolate to share, Christmas trees to decorate together, and the delight of finding the perfect gift for the one you love. All the Hallmark movies can leave you feeling that you are missing out on the joys of the season because of your singleness. Let's change this narrative! Start your own traditions and learn to make the most of each season — alone or with friends. One of my favorite Christmas traditions is with two of my single friends. On Christmas Eve, we attend the church service together, go to Dairy Queen for candy cane Blizzards, and then drive around to see Christmas lights. It has become a fun tradition. Choose to see the holidays as a time to be joyful. Walk confidently into them, knowing that you have the freedom to enjoy them fully.

Free to Enjoy Weddings

Whether it is June, December, or any other month, love is always in the air. In a world of "I do" and "plus one," we can find ourselves saying "I don't" and "plus none." How do you navigate a wedding by yourself? I have been to countless weddings without a plus one. They can be just as fun by yourself as they would be with a date.

Be confident. Having a date or not having a date does not change who you are. You are a daughter of the King. Slip on your heels, apply your lipstick, and hold your head up high. You are beautiful!

At weddings, be on the lookout for other single girls who may feel the same way you do. Is there a single girl sitting by herself at the reception? Invite her to sit with you, or go sit with her! Start the conversation. And when the Cha Cha Slide comes on, definitely get out there on the dance floor. (Okay, but for real, when it comes to tossing the bouquet, push all those other girls out of the way, and go for it. No shame).

If weddings truly cause discontentment in your heart, purpose to change that. When you start to feel jealous, *pray*. Pray and share your desires with God. Ask Him for a godly husband. Ask Him for joy for the season you are in. When you start to feel resentment, *praise*. Start thanking God for all the great things that come with this season right now.

Living the Life Wisely

Singleness is a great time to start building lifelong habits. Your habits of overspending or overeating are not magically going to go away when you get married. Today's choices make you into tomorrow's decision maker. So how are you going to live? What person are you going to be today? Tomorrow?

Free to Save

With regard to money management or mismanagement when you are single, nobody knows. No one knows how much is on that credit card. No one knows if you spent $200 on a new look. No one will know if you are obedient in tithing. No one will know if you have a humble, giving spirit.

No one. Except God.

So how are you with your money? Are you buying things outside your means? Spending too much? God calls us as His children to be different. Romans 13:8 says, "Let no debt remain outstanding, except the continuing debt to love one another, for whoever loves others has fulfilled the law" (NIV). When the shopaholic tendencies overtake you and the desire to overstuff your wardrobe seems more than you can handle, go out and do for others. Get your focus off of what you do not have and love on others.

Do you overwork yourself to hoard away money? Always checking your bank account? Hate when you feel pressured to spend or give money to others? Ecclesiastes 5:10 says, "Whoever loves money never has enough; whoever loves wealth is never satisfied with their income. This too is meaningless" (NIV). You will never be satisfied. Ask God for a giving heart. Ask Him to show you how you can use your resources to bless others. It's hard. It's not easy to live differently than how others around you are living. My pastor says of discipline that "We can choose discipline now or regret will choose us later."

Finances were an area in my life where I didn't think I struggled. To be honest, I really didn't even think about finances that much. I just knew that I had this bill due then and that much money in my bank and "Oh that dress is only $19.99? Well, why not?" My friend Elizabeth and I decided to take a Financial Peace University class a few years ago, and the knowledge I gained from that class changed my life. I realized the intentionality I could be having with my money and how I could better walk in obedience in this area. So I made a budget and started making changes in my thinking and in my decisions.

Every day I would pray over my finances because I knew I needed help from the Holy Spirit. I also had an accountability partner to keep me in check and to review my monthly budget. Was the discipline hard? Yes. Was it always fun? No. Discipline is painful, but it will eventually yield peace and fruit.

Elizabeth went on to pay off $38,000 in student loans in fourteen months and buy her first home. She had intense discipline — working three jobs and saying no to many things. I was also able to pay off my student loans and car loan by being intentional and disciplined. The fruit and the peace of our hard work eventually came.

Stereotypically, handling finances is an area with which many women in a season of singleness struggle. I believe this is either because of a lack of knowledge or because spending becomes a way to fill emptiness or medicate pain. God is asking you to choose what is wisest for the long term rather than what feels good now.

If handling finances is an area where you lack discipline or knowledge, do something about it. Look for a Financial Peace class in your area.[3] Start reading and researching online. Get an accountability partner. Create a budget. Don't allow money to keep you from experiencing freedom — freedom to give, to travel, to love others well, to not be bound to a loan or a credit card payment. Be content and thank God for what you have. Hebrews 13:5 says, "Keep your lives free from the love of money and be content with what you have, because God has said, 'Never will I leave you; never will I forsake you'" (NIV).

Living the Life Freely

A word of caution with this chapter: while singleness is a season to live life freely, it is not to be freely wasted. It is not a season of narcissism. It is not a season to craft the perfect Instagram profile nor to binge-watch your favorite shows every night. It is not a season to spend away, numb away, or scroll away your loneliness. I often hear single women say, "This is time for me; I get to do whatever I want to do. I'm just focused on me right now."

You should be "focused on me" in the sense of deepening your relationship with Jesus, building godly habits of prayer, being in the Word, and becoming more like Jesus. Singleness should be a season of selflessness. This should be a season of being concerned about the things of the Lord. This should be a season of being holy in your body — what you eat, drink, and do sexually. This should be a season of being holy in your spirit — what you love, think about, and spend time on.

Jesus lived a single life, selflessly devoted to you and me. He gave His life so that you and I could go free. Paul lived unmarried, dedicated to discipling the church. How will you choose to live out your singleness?

Singleness is a season to live free. Don't be bound to discontent, waiting, debt, or selfishness. Instead, live as you were called to live — free. Travel, go to concerts, have fun; but ultimately, use your freedom to love and serve others.

SCENE 5

The Tragedy of Heartbreak

Maybe you wanted your script to be a romance. The one where the damsel in distress is saved and whisked away by the handsome hero. Or maybe you were eyeing the comedy script where life is fun and light. Instead, it's looking like you were assigned to play the lead role in a tragedy — the one where the main character experiences all kinds of hurt and pain and is left all alone at the end.

Life can feel like that sometimes. It can feel as if you were handed the wrong script. You auditioned for one role and ended up with another. So how do you see joy in the midst of the script you were given? How do you see the love of the Author Who is writing your part? Grab a tissue and be prepared because there is no acting when it comes to dealing with pain.

Rejection

"It's over."

"I want to break up with you."

"I can't anymore."

"I'm not really interested."

"I don't feel the same way I felt before."

Rejected. If you have dated for any length of time or put yourself out there at all in the dating world, you have probably heard these words or something similar to them. What do you do with these words? How do you process words you didn't want to hear?

Fellowship of Sufferings

Find comfort in this: you are not alone in feeling rejected. I can totally identify with you. I've been rejected. I've been broken up with. I've been led on. And it *hurts*. The unexpected heartbreak wounds you deeply. Many other sisters around you are raising their hands saying, "I have felt rejection too." It can be comforting knowing that others have also played this role and have experienced healing on the other side.

The greatest comfort above all is that Jesus doesn't leave you alone in your sufferings. I remember meeting with my mentor after experiencing rejection, and her response blew me away: "I don't know how it feels to be in your shoes and to be rejected by a boyfriend, but I do know how it feels to be rejected. More so, though, Christ knows how it feels to be rejected." The most reassuring part of shared sufferings is knowing that the One Who has the answers to our hurt and pain has felt rejection too.

Share in the Sufferings of Christ

Paul's "goal is to know Him and the power of His resurrection and the *fellowship of His sufferings*, being conformed to His death" (Philippians 3:10 HCSB, emphasis added). If we are honest, we only want to know Christ in the power of His resurrection. We don't want the struggles and hard situations in our lives; we only want victory and mountain-top praise. But since we live in a broken world, we will experience pain and suffering until we are with Jesus. My mentor helped me see that one important way of knowing Him is through the fellowship of His sufferings. I can rejoice in difficulties in my life, not just because of the good they produce (James 1:2-4; Romans 5:3-5), but because it is a way of knowing my Jesus better.

Here's an example from a different perspective. My mom has Multiple Sclerosis. It is not who she is, but it plays a huge part in what she does. If I only wanted to be around her when she is happy and free of struggle, our relationship would not be very deep. However, it is being with her in her suffering and pain that deepens our bond and allows me to know her on another level. It is the same with Jesus. I can't only choose to identify with Him in a few ways. Jesus wants us to intimately know Him in every way.

He knows the feelings of pain and rejection because of what He endured on earth. Hebrews 4:15 reminds us, "For we do not have a high priest who is unable to sympathize with our weaknesses, but one who in every respect has been tempted as we are, yet without sin" (ESV). He can empathize with us and comfort us. It is like having a friend walk alongside you, put her arm around you, and say, "I've been there. It hurts. I know your pain." Because she has experienced similar circumstances and feelings, she can comfort you in a way unlike someone who has never suffered as you have. It is the same with Jesus. 2 Corinthians 1:7b brings great encouragement "for we know that as you share in our sufferings, so you will share in our comfort" (ESV).

We are heirs with Christ. How? By suffering with Him. Romans 8:17 says, "And if children, then heirs — heirs of God and fellow heirs with Christ, *provided we suffer with him* in order that we may also be glorified with him" (ESV, emphasis added). Suffering will happen. But so will the reward. Wait for it. Wait for your inheritance patiently. The full reward will come one day when we see Jesus, but learn to recognize the rewards He has given you here on earth — namely, knowing Him and looking more like Him. What a priceless gift accompanies the role He has chosen for you!

In what ways does Jesus understand our hurt? Isaiah 53:3 tells us that "He was despised and rejected by men, a man of sorrows and acquainted with grief; and as one from whom men hide their faces he was despised, and we esteemed him not" (ESV). People walked away from Jesus, deeming His words and presence inconsequential. He felt rejection from the religious. He was scorned by His enemies. Some people hated Jesus so much that they wanted Him murdered. Even His trusted friends and disciples abandoned Jesus in the most difficult of hours.

When we experience feelings of rejection, we can take them to Jesus and say, "You know how this feels. In fact, I have even caused You to feel these feelings because I have rejected You many times. I have despised You, yet You loved me! I will praise You because I can know You better through this suffering. I can know more of what You endured to show me Your love. Thank you, Jesus." Even though you rejected Christ initially, He has not rejected you. He accepts you. What a beautiful pursuit of love by our God!

In your heartbreak, change your perspective to be like Paul's and know Him more by the fellowship of His sufferings.

Dealing with Hurt

Even though you know Christ and others have also walked the road of rejection, it doesn't take away the pain. You still have to deal with the hurt. When rejection comes, allow yourself to process and experience grief. Cry. Express your frustrations to God in journal entries. Share your heart over coffee with a trusted friend.

As a happy-go-lucky person, I wrestle with processing difficult or negative emotions because to me, life is meant for happiness and fun. A few years ago, I experienced rejection from a guy I was interested in. My hope had been deferred, and I was devastated. Normally, I would stuff down the emotions and lie to myself, saying, "I never really cared that much anyway. I am fine. I am better off now." But the Lord had been working in my heart and in my emotions, and I decided to intentionally take a few days to grieve, cry, write down my raw thoughts, and deal with the pain. All the hurt didn't go away right then, but acknowledging the pain and allowing myself a specific time to grieve helped me to process how I felt rather than distracting myself or ignoring the feelings. I took long walks and shed many tears. I called friends and cried on the phone with them. It was healthy for me to process the hurt.

Honesty with yourself and with God is the first step to healing. Part of allowing yourself to process the rejection is being real and admitting how you feel. The Lord is still growing me in this area. When feelings and memories of pain arise, I make it a point to acknowledge them to God rather than stuff them or ignore them. I candidly share with Him, "I am feeling _____ right now because _____." In the rejection, I realized my frustration toward God; I felt betrayed and wounded by Him. The good thing was that I brought those feelings to Him. I struggled *toward* God, not *away* from Him. God wants to hear your heart. Read the Psalms. In many of them, David deals with afflictions and questioning God. (For a starting point, read and journal through Psalm 25 and Psalm 40.)

Perhaps you fall on the "overly emotional" side of things. I would advise the same process. Cry and grieve. At some point, however, you need to get up from wallowing and move on. The hurt won't magically go away, but you cannot sit on it and in it and expect things to change. Time with God and being in His Word will bring healing.

Find friends with whom you can be honest. When they ask you how you are doing, don't give an "I'm fine" response. Romans 12:15b instructs the body of Christ to "weep with those who weep" (ESV). Allow the body to step in and help comfort you. I struggle with this because I would rather help others than be helped. Holding things in isn't how God created us to deal with pain. God gave us a community of people to help us when we are going through a difficult time.

I love the emotion Jesus expressed when He came to be with Mary and Martha after the death of Lazarus. "When Jesus saw her weeping, and the Jews who had come along with her also weeping, he was deeply moved in spirit and troubled . . . Jesus wept" (John 11:33, 35 NIV). Jesus comes into a community of people weeping together, knowing He will raise Lazarus from the dead. Yet Jesus is still overcome with emotion at the sight of His beloved friends hurting. And that's what Jesus feels when He sees your pain and mine. He knows the good that will come from the hurt, yet He still weeps with us. Allow others to weep with you too, Sister.

Above all, seek holiness in your hurting. Don't go to food (I'm talking about that pint of Halo Top Chocolate Peanut Butter or Ben & Jerry's Cookie Dough) or withdraw from it. Don't go to anger. Don't go to self-harm. Don't go to bitter and hateful words.

Do go to God's Word. Do allow His truth to shape your suffering. Do appreciate the beauty of pain in a way this world doesn't understand. Do remind yourself that this heartbreak doesn't define you. If you find yourself drawn to destructive behaviors, seek help from a biblical counselor or mentor.

Don't Claim Feelings as Fact

The feeling of rejection is true; however, the feeling itself is not truth. You cannot deny the feelings. You do have to work through them, but do not let these feelings define you. You may *feel* rejected but your *identity* is not rejected. God calls you chosen, redeemed, set apart (1 Peter 2:9), and purposely planned before time began (Ephesians 2:10). A good way to process feelings versus fact is to write down how you feel in one column and write down what God says about you in the other. Claim the truth not the emotion. "Whatever is true . . . dwell on these things" (Philippians 4:8 HCSB).

The Good in the Pain

After several difficult years in my early 20s, I finally settled into an overall state of contentment with my singleness. It had been years since I had dated, and I was focusing on serving God and living my best single life. Out of nowhere, I met a guy and started to hope again. I started to dream that God might truly have marriage for me. I had pushed those thoughts aside because I did not want to risk being disappointed by God. But then someone who I actually considered a possibility came into my life. He checked all the boxes. Just when I started allowing my heart to open up to the desire of marriage again, he realized he didn't see me that way anymore. He confessed that he probably should have never said the things he said, and he was no longer interested. *Rejected.* My hopes were dashed. The first part of Proverbs 13:12 says that "delayed hope makes the heart sick" (HCSB), and I felt physically sick. It was as if someone sucker punched me in the stomach and knocked the wind out of me. The rejection, mistrust, pain, and hurt all piled up into tight knots in my back. I was honest with God, crying out, "Why did You mess with me!? Why did You disrupt my contentment?!"

But God brought so much good out of that pain. The rest of that verse says "but fulfilled desire is a tree of life." For this situation, I would have thought that fulfilled desire would mean a boyfriend or marriage. But Jesus knew the desire was greater — the desire to be completely known and loved. He wanted me to see that He is that Desire-Filler. He is the Tree of life, and the life He gave on the tree on Golgotha gives us a hope and a future. This earth will always have delayed hopes, but Jesus is the only desire that will truly fulfill us.

This pain also led to experiencing His love in unimaginable ways. I came to know Him more intimately through the suffering and rejection. The truth of how He knows and loves me washed over me in ways like never before. God also used this rejection to prompt me to start my singleness blog — Singled Out for Him — and to write this book.

Ultimately, God made me more like Him. Nick Person, the teaching pastor at my church, says, "There are things that can only be built through the refining fire of suffering." I think about the difficulties of a relationship ending and the pain of a broken heart. It's easy for me to say, "Why? Couldn't I have avoided this? I wish I hadn't allowed myself to hope for this relationship. Does God even care about my heart? Why would He allow me to hope for — or even give me peace about — this relationship only to have it end?" But I can look back and see God's grace and sanctification in the pain. I look a little bit more like Jesus because of the heartbreak. I understand people a little better and can put my arm around another crying sister and say, "I have been there too." I ran to Jesus and felt His closeness and presence, deepening my trust in Him.

God is kind, even in the pain. He wants to show you Himself in this broken world. If you are still healing or hurting from a relationship, pray and ask God to show you His purpose and how you are becoming more like Jesus. Then raise your hands in thanksgiving and praise Him in the midst of it all.

Ghosted

There's the rejection of a relationship that has closure and parting words, even ones that really hurt. Then there's the rejection that comes from no closure and no parting words but rather an abrupt ending. This means you have just been ghosted. Being ghosted is "when someone you're dating ends the relationship by cutting off all communication, without any explanation . . . receiving the ultimate silent treatment after several dates, or when you're in a committed relationship."[1]

I had just gone out with this guy and had a fun time. We had been talking for a few weeks, and he finally asked me out. He confirmed before we parted ways that he also had a great time and followed with "Let's do it again soon!" Then I heard nothing for days. A week later, I saw him at a church activity, and he completely ignored me. This confirmed what I had begun to realize. I had just been ghosted.

What in the world happened over those few days? I was hurt. And mad. I would rather have him be honest and just tell me he was not interested. It helps to have some closure rather than questions and no answers.

So I texted a close friend about my frustrations along with the perfect ghosting meme. After we confirmed how much of a jerk he was and how he didn't deserve me anyway (you know, all the things a good friend says), my friend centered me back on truth. She reminded me, "Lauren, you are loved — by God and by those around you. Don't let one guy's actions toward you dictate how you view yourself, much less feel about yourself. I don't know what happened, and I understand why you're feeling the way you are. But I also know that you are learning and growing. Maybe this happened just so you would submit to God's control in your life over what you want. I have seen that submission playing out in your life." It was just the truth and encouragement I needed. So I got out my journal and wrote down several things that I had learned from this ghosting experience.

Author and speaker Leighann McCoy (wish we were related, but we are not) said, "You *will* have trouble, but you *can* have peace." Trouble is guaranteed as Jesus tells His followers in John 16:33, but peace is a choice. Believing what God says is a choice. Rejoicing in rejection is a choice. We *can* choose to do this.

Boo! Ghosting is not ghoul (sorry not sorry for the bad puns). If you ever find yourself being ghosted, remind yourself of truth. Pick yourself up and find yourself at the feet of Jesus — the One Who will never leave us nor forsake us. Praise Jesus for this promise!

Choose Your Interpretation
So when you are ghosted or rejected . . .

> *Choose to see it as God protecting you from something other than His best.* What if you never experienced the pain of the rejection but instead faced the pain from which God wanted to protect you?

> *Choose to see it as good from God.* "And we know that for those who love God all things work together for

good, for those who are called according to his purpose" (Romans 8:28 ESV).

Choose to see it as God working in you. "And not only that, but we also rejoice in our afflictions, because we know that affliction produces endurance, endurance produces proven character, and proven character produces hope" (Romans 5:3-4 HCSB).

Choose to see it as God wanting you to know Him. "My goal is to know Him and the power of His resurrection and the fellowship of His sufferings" (Philippians 3:10a HCSB).

How are you going to look at your script when rejection comes? Don't wallow in it, thinking your play to be a tragedy. Embrace laughter and choose to see parts as a comedy. Play the Proverbs 31 leading woman who laughs at the time to come (Proverbs 31:25). Interpret your story as a romance where the Lover of your soul woos you back to Himself. You get to choose how you play the part.

ACT II

The Supporting Actors

SCENE 6
Dating

Dating. Blind dates. Online dating. Red flags. Standards. Awkwardness. Meet the family. You may often find yourself in one particular scene of the singleness script: the dating scene. It might be the most fun part to be in, but it also just might be the hardest. The stress of dating can be overwhelming. Everyone's dating journey is different, and navigating your own journey will require much prayer and wisdom from God and others.

Prepare for Dating
Be Open
The first step to dating is to let go of the concept of the ideal man. He is not out there. You need to be open to dat-

ing and to appreciating different types of guys. You may never know with whom you actually pair best if you aren't open and willing to get to know someone.

One time I almost said no to a first date. A family friend had messaged me on Facebook wanting to set me up with "this guy" from her church. Her description of him didn't match up with someone with whom I had envisioned myself. All of the qualities she mentioned were great, yet they didn't quite suit the type of guy I had pictured in my mind. When I shared with my parents that I was planning to tell her I was not interested, they encouraged me to go. "Lauren, it's a first date! It is only fair to at least give him a chance." So I went on the date with the thought in the back of my mind that maybe I could set him up with one of my friends who seemed to fit more with "this type" of guy.

And then he piqued my interest. He intrigued me. He was different from anyone else I had ever met. I walked away thinking, "Hmm . . . that was not what I was expecting at all." I wanted to know more. I wanted to spend more time getting to know him. So I did.

The Lord started revealing to me that I was being held back by my "certain type of man" idea, and it was causing me to miss out on getting to know guys who truly had potential to capture my heart. We went on to date for almost a year. While things didn't work out with him in the long run, I learned to be open to brothers-in-Christ regardless of preconceived notions. People who have different backgrounds or interests can add depth to your life and open your eyes to new perspectives.

I love the advice Jamal Miller, a dating expert, gave on an episode of the Heart of Dating podcast. "Divorce the woman or man in your head. [Don't] weigh [the person in front of you] up against the person that you believe you are supposed to be with. Give that person the chance to build their case, and get to know them for who they are versus comparing them to a person you may never even meet."[1]

In a world of Instagram perfection, don't let the person you have created in your mind close your heart to considering quality guys. Let go of expectations of how your ideal man should look. Jesus doesn't judge us on our looks but rather on our hearts. We should be more concerned about the heart than the appearance too. Be open. As a friend of mine likes to say, "God loves to surprise!"

Types of Dating
Blind Dates

While some people might shy away from being set up, I say, "Go for it." At least give it a try. My mom and dad met on a blind date, and I have met many great guys on blind dates as well. If you trust the people who are setting you up, it might just be the best way to meet someone.

Blind dates can definitely be nerve racking, though. We often put so much pressure on the first date and first impressions that it can make a nervous wreck out of us. So how do you prepare? Let's go back to a first date I had recently. (Remember the one I just told you I almost didn't go on? It was that guy.)

I was in my bathroom getting ready for the date, butterflies fluttering in my stomach, when I was reminded of some wise words I had heard on a podcast by dating expert Kait Warman. She said that our number one reason for dating should be to reflect God through our actions and the actions of our dating lives. Making glorifying God the number one reason for dating helps the expectations and pressures fall away. We start to see that this could actually be a time of edifying a brother, a time that is not about us but about God and His purposes.

So as I was putting on my make-up, I started praying for my blind date. I prayed that he would leave our time together more encouraged in his faith. I asked God that my date would see Jesus in my life. I prayed he would grow in his walk and as a man after God's heart.

I decided to see him as a brother-in-Christ and not as a "potential."

This focus of prayer for him and the renewed purpose of why I was even going on the date calmed me down and gave me a greater peace and confidence that only comes from talking to Jesus. Next time you go on a first date or second date or third, pray for the guy you are dating. Make it a goal to encourage him in Christ.

Online Dating

Online dating or dating via app is the trendy way to meet people these days. This isn't surprising since we are such a "connected" society. While I personally have never tried any sort of online dating (not due to personal convictions — I just never had any interest), I have several friends who have gone this route. A few of them are now married to someone they met online.

In answering the question of whether to date online or not, John Piper responded by saying, "The biblical issue here is not how you meet, but whom you marry."[2] The importance here is not *how* you choose to meet someone. The importance is concerning *whom* you choose to marry. So for those of you who are scared that online dating is bad, may this perspective bring freedom.

Here are some things to think through with online dating:

> *Be mindful of your emotions.* It can seem like you are on a rollercoaster. It can become game-like or a means to get the thrill of the chase without having the commitment. You could find yourself on the doing or receiving end of this.

Be cognizant of the crafted perfection you see and the perfection you portray. Everyone wants the best profile pic and the best descriptions. Keep in mind that there is always more to the story. Nobody is perfect.

Know that commitment can be hard to come by. This is true of our generation in general, but I would say it is magnified in the online dating platform where ghosting is the norm.

Stand firm in your convictions and in sexual integrity. This goes for any dating — online or not.

Keep yourself accountable. Have someone ask you hard questions about your accounts or what you are doing and saying on the apps.

Be aware if it gets unhealthy. I have several friends who delete their apps when they know they are in a lonely place or only seeking affirmation.

Know the reputations and expectations of the apps you choose. Some apps have the association of being a means to hookup. Stay clear of the ones that don't align with your values and beliefs.

Don't let it consume you. Dating apps, like any app, can become addictive and another means of scrolling and liking. If you find yourself spending too much time on them, set time restrictions on your phone in the settings.

Before you jump onto a dating app, know your motivating factor for doing so. Pray and be accountable to others along the way.

Officially Dating
Prepare for Pain

If you want a happy, pain-free life, don't date. Relationships come with great joy and adventure, but they also come with deep pain and heartache. C.S. Lewis says,

> To love at all is to be vulnerable. Love anything and your heart will be wrung and possibly broken. If you want to make sure of keeping it intact you must give it to no one, not even an animal. Wrap it carefully round with hobbies and little luxuries; avoid all entanglements. Lock it up safe in the casket or coffin of your selfishness. But in that casket, safe, dark, motionless, airless, it will change. It will not be broken; it will become unbreakable, impenetrable, irredeemable. To love is to be vulnerable.[3]

If you want a relationship, you must be willing to take the risk of being hurt because dating involves two broken people.

Proverbs 4:23 instructs us, "Above all else, guard your heart, for everything you do flows from it" (NIV). What a beautiful and wise verse! But what if we are misapplying it to our love lives? The context of this verse is a man instructing his son to pursue wisdom and live a righteous life. I believe he is saying to guard what you allow into your heart — what you think about, watch, treasure, long for, etc. I have often heard this verse used as a way to avoid the pain of a relationship.

"I'm guarding my heart" leads to saying no to that first date. It gives the excuse for not wanting to take the chance of transitioning from going on dates to a committed relationship because the last time that happened, I was hurt. We avoid the struggles and differences that naturally come with a relationship because they are difficult and take hard work. It is easy to keep people at a safe distance. The phrase "guarding our hearts" becomes a cop-out to protect ourselves from the risk of rejection.

Does that mean to throw your heart at any man who will give you attention? Absolutely not. Always pursue wisdom when dating. Just don't guard your heart in a way that strives to protect yourself at all costs. What if Christ guarded His heart from us? We break His heart all the time. However, the rich love that comes from a soft brokenness outweighs the safety of the impenetrable, unbreakable heart in a casket. Guard your heart against the loves of the world while opening up your heart to be loved and to love others.

The Type of Man You Date

My mom always says, "Stop looking for a John Piper. John Piper is in his 70s." What she means is that so many of us women are passing by godly men because our perspective is that they don't measure up to the influential men in our lives: our fathers, grandfathers, pastors, etc. These men, years older than the men I would date, have been through refining times that have made them into the God-fearing men that they are.

Now this advice does not allow for "missionary dating" or dating someone who is an unbeliever in order to win them to Christ. God commands us not to date or marry into this circumstance (2 Corinthians 6:14). Being a believer of Jesus Christ is non-negotiable.

You should see certain qualities in a man before you continue dating him. Here are three overarching characteristics I look for in a potential mate:

1) He is a believer who seeks to love God above all else.
2) He is faithful in being with a community of believers and being in the Word.
3) Spending time with him is sanctifying, and I walk away wanting more of Jesus.

If a man is living out these characteristics, I believe he is a godly man worthy of pursuing you. Don't hold your brothers-in-Christ to an impossible standard. Above all, see if they are chasing after Jesus because that is what really matters.

The List

The List. It was such a big thing when I was in middle and high school. For those unfamiliar with this concept, *The List* consisted of characteristics girls wanted and longed for in a future husband. Just like it is easy to be caught up looking for a John Piper, we can also tend to only look for a man who checks off all the things on our list.

I dug my list out of my crate of journals the other day and ... oh, my! Part of me thought, "Wow! Impressive insight, seventh-grade Lauren;" and the other part of me cringed, "Lauren, you definitely exhibit the mind and emotions of a seventh grader." I had included over ninety things on *The List. Nine zero.* And we find the Ten Commandments hard to keep! Lord have mercy on my future spouse!

The List had everything from the insightful seventh-grade Lauren — willing to admit when he's wrong, honest, has God first in His life, growing in Christ — to the emotional and hormonal middle-school Lauren — dresses nice, can cook (Am I trying to make this too hard for myself?!), has good hair (I'm lucky if any have hair at this age), smells good (no comment), etc.

My friends and I were recently debating the value of *The List* we had created in high school. My initial reaction was to do away with it completely, mostly due to the ridiculous characteristics I had written down. But then I considered my middle school self and applauded what God was doing. He was instilling in me godly desires for a man who resembles Himself and who will lead me.

What I see now as a single woman in my 20s is that marriage is not about the extra things that I think I need — those things that fulfill all my desires and longings. It's okay to have preferences and to be attracted to certain things, but I needed to realize that these are not deal breakers. Our concept of what we want is incredibly different from what God wants for us and what He knows we need.

Society and movies set us up to wait for "The Perfect Man" to waltz into our lives with roses and a charming smile. Pastor Nick once shared a quote that highlights the damage that can come from these fanciful thoughts. "Unrealistic expectations always lead to disappointment . . . Lofty expectations are premeditated resentments."[4] We meditate on what the movies tell us guys should do (those flowers, chocolates, shopping trips, and mushy words) and what guys should look like (tall, dark, and handsome). When God brings a godly guy who intensely pursues Jesus into our lives, we either dismiss him because he doesn't look like what we envisioned (remember — be open!), or we start a relationship with him while holding onto a tiny bit of resentment because he doesn't meet our unrealistic expectations.

On the other side of this are women who start knocking important things off their non-negotiable list as they get older and their desire for marriage intensifies. When you are fifteen, *The List* is set. You would never settle for anyone not checking all the boxes. At twenty-five, you are beginning to lose hope and edit *The List*. It would just be nice to have a good man who goes to church and has a consistent job. At thirty-five, desperation sets in. You are okay with a man who has been to church at least one time in his life and can quote a few verses. *The List* is now completely disregarded.[5] This may be a bit exaggerated and hopefully not true in your case, but I think the principle can be true.

A list of biblical non-negotiables can be valuable. With this list, though, understand that no one is perfect. Pastor Nick also says, "Marriage is made up of two people still in process." Understand that this man you are dating or considering dating is in a process. The test should be — where is that process heading? Is it headed toward himself? Is it headed toward ambition? Is it headed toward the world? Or is he in a process headed toward Christ? Is it headed toward dying to himself daily? Pray and seek counsel about these characteristics on your biblical non-negotiable list. Allow the process to be God-focused and

Spirit-led. Marriage is 'til death do us part. It is serious. But it is also a free-will decision from God that allows us freedom in choosing.

The Perfect Man

If you find someone you like and begin dating more intentionally, you may find yourself asking, "Is he the perfect person for me?" Marshall Segal writes,

> Many of us need to be reminded that God's perfect person for me isn't all that perfect. Every person who marries is a sinner, so the search for a spouse isn't a pursuit of perfection, but a mutually flawed pursuit of Jesus. . . . We probably need to be reminded that marriage really is less about compatibility than commitment. After all, there has never been a less compatible relationship than a holy God and his sinful bride, and that's the mold we're aiming for in our marriages.[6]

This truth opens the door for grace to enter into the relationship. The more you get to know the man you are dating, the more you will see his sin struggles and the more he will see yours. But we are not looking for a perfect man. We already have a perfect Man in Jesus. Look for a man who is committed to God, committed to you, and committed to becoming more like Jesus in your potential marriage. When sin is revealed in his life or your life, God gives us the opportunity to offer grace and truth to each other like Jesus offers us.

Remember: Don't look for the perfect man. That expectation is met only by Jesus. Instead, look for a man who will pursue Jesus with you.

Red Flags

Red flags are warning signs and behaviors indicating that something needs to be questioned or otherwise explained. They give you a sense that something is not right. It is important to look for red flags in relationships. They cause you to reevaluate things.

We know we aren't looking for a perfect man, but where is the line? You certainly don't want to marry a man who has no care for God or who has explosive anger or waves other red flags. But I wonder how many of the red flags that we see in the men we are dating could actually just be *yellow* flags? Pastor Brady once said to look for "progress over perfection." Don't look for or expect perfection; rather, expect progress and growth. Consider: is this man growing and pursuing Christ in the areas of his weakness and struggle?

We all come with our own yellow flags (or perhaps even red flags). A man could look at my yellow flags of fear, control, pride, and self-righteousness and call them red flags; but I hope that instead he will see how Christ is working in my life in these areas. Progress over perfection. Is the man you are considering as a potential mate portraying perfection? Only Jesus is perfect. Is this man revealing his areas of weakness and struggle while progressing in his walk with the Lord? Meet him with grace. Is he acknowledging his sin and doing nothing about it or even boasting about it? Those are red flags waving. Just remember that Jesus meets us as repentant sinners with grace and mercy; therefore, we should meet other repentant sinners the same way.

Living with Sexual Integrity
God's Will for Your Sex Life

God has a beautiful design and purpose for your sex life. Sex was created by God and is a good gift. In Eden, before sin entered, Adam and Eve enjoyed the freedom of God's design. "Therefore a man shall leave his father and his mother and hold fast to his wife, and they shall become one flesh. And the man and his wife were both naked and were not ashamed" (Genesis 2:24-25 ESV). This sinless marriage before the Fall was founded on unity between husband and wife. They were naked together without shame. They enjoyed freedom, intimacy, and companionship. Sex was intended to build harmony and unity within a marriage relationship. It is a picture of the intimacy God longs to have with His Bride, the Church.

Enter sin. "Then the eyes of both were opened, and they knew that they were naked. And they sewed fig leaves together and made themselves loincloths" (Genesis 3:7 ESV). The openness and freedom was broken, shattered into shame and hiding that continues today. Sex has been misused ever since the Fall — sex without consent, adultery, pornography, sex slavery, sex outside of marriage, using sex or lack of sex to manipulate a spouse, prostitution, and many more ways. Satan has whispered lies that result in covering up with loincloths and sewn fig leaves. "Sex is bad. Sex is fun. You can do it whenever and with whomever you feel like doing it. Sex is gross. It is your body and your decision. You can please yourself. You don't need commitment or a man."

Sex, in and of itself, is not wrong. Sex was not a result of the Fall. It was a part of creation before sin entered and is therefore good. We were created as sexual beings. God uniquely created the bodies of men and women with sexual organs intended specifically for sex. Sex is not gross. It is a holy, God-created, and God-gifted thing. God desires restoration and sexual integrity for His Church. He wants His people to enjoy sex in the way He designed, with a Garden-like intimacy: husband and wife, nakedness, one flesh, no shame.

God's "sex between a husband and wife" is a means of protection. He wants us to experience the joy and sacredness of covenant-bound sex. It is true that the consequences from sexual choices affect us in deep ways. Paul, in I Corinthians 6:18, warns us, "Flee from sexual immorality. Every other sin a person commits is outside the body, but the sexually immoral person sins against his own body" (ESV).

Since sex is for marriage, how are we to live sexually as women in a season of singleness? God's will for your sexual life is outlined in I Thessalonians 4:3-7:

> For this is the will of God, your sanctification: that you abstain from sexual immorality; that each one of you know how to control his own body in holiness and honor, not in the passion of lust like the Gentiles who do not know God; that no one transgress and wrong his brother in this matter, because the Lord is an avenger in all these things, as we told you beforehand and solemnly warned you. For God has not called us for impurity, but in holiness (ESV).

Pursuing sexual integrity[7] is a means of sanctification or being made more like Christ in holiness. God's will is for us to control our bodies in holiness and honor. Paul is telling the Thessalonians that the way we live sexually is a testimony to the world. We should be different in our choices. When we live outside of God's design for sex, we are living like unbelievers.

God has outlined His sexual will for your life. Will you follow it? Will you be sanctified by setting aside your desires for His desires? You are a daughter of the King, and your body is a temple of the Holy Spirit. Walk in honor, dignity, and sexual integrity.

What's the Standard?

God's design is for sex to be within the covenant of marriage. This leaves a lot of gray area and can have you asking the ongoing popular question: "How far is too far?" Personally, I want a black-and-white answer. I would rather the standard be "This is ok, and this is not." My proud, rule-following heart would do my best to check all of the boxes and self-righteously pat myself on the back.

But Jesus sets a higher standard than a list of dos and don'ts. It is not a list of rules or behaviors to be kept. The standard starts in the heart. "You have heard that it was said, 'You shall not commit adultery.' But I tell you that anyone who looks at a woman lustfully has already committed adultery with her in his heart" (Matthew 5:27-28 NIV).

Jesus is challenging the righteous and the pious — those who look down upon others committing physical acts of sin. Jesus calls them out — He calls *us* out — and levels the field. They are all guilty. *We* are all guilty. If you have lusted in your heart, it is the same as committing the sin. Jesus' standard of sexual wholeness echoes within the story of the woman caught in adultery. The righteous men standing around were ready to stone her for her sin. But Jesus said, "Let any one of you who is without sin be the first to throw a stone at her" (John 8:7b NIV). None of them could throw a stone because they were, like we are, guilty of lust and sin.

Dr. Juli Slattery reminds us that "God doesn't see us in categories of our sexuality. He sees His beloved creation, deceived by sin and rebellious in nature."[8] Just because you are a virgin does not mean you are sexually sinless. We are all guilty. We all come with a past of sexual sins and a current struggle for sexual integrity. Romans 3:23 says, "For all have sinned and fall short of the glory of God" (NIV).

So what is the standard? Purity. Purity in your actions; but, more importantly, purity in your heart and mind.

No one can keep this standard of purity because our hearts are deceitful and desperately wicked (Jeremiah 17:9). This measure of sexual wholeness reveals our need for Jesus to create a new heart within us. It calls for the renewal of our minds so we can know what is good and acceptable (Romans 12:2). How intensely must we seek the Lord! Only His Holy Spirit can renew our hearts and minds and help us pursue true holiness and sexual integrity.

After realizing the need for purity within your heart and mind, take some time to think through sexual boundaries you want to set for yourself and your relationships. It is wise to set practical boundaries. What guidelines can you set for yourself to help you avoid sinning physically and mentally? When discussing boundaries, my friend Elizabeth and her boyfriend asked each other these questions: "What makes you want to do more sexually? What makes you feel uncomfortable physically? What causes you to think impure thoughts?" Know your boundaries and the boundaries of the person you are dating and seek accountability.

When I was seriously dating a guy, I created a list of questions for accountability and texted them to Elizabeth. I would let her know when my boyfriend and I were hanging out. At the end of the day, she would always text me those questions. Having those boundaries and her accountability helped me strive to walk in purity within that relationship.

When you are dating and trying to figure out "how far" or what the standard is, pray this daily: *"Lord, create in me a clean heart. Help me not to seek outward conformity only. Rather, first and foremost, remove the lust from within my heart. Replace it with the purity and wholeness of Christ's righteousness. Renew my mind with your truth so I can discern what is good and acceptable. Lead me and order my steps."*

Healing

What I love about the Bible is that God uses all people — the beautiful Queen Esther, the faithful virgin Mary, the redeemed prostitute Rahab, the demon-possessed Mary Magdalene, the widowed Ruth, the old and barren Sarah, the despondent woman at the well, and many more.

While it's easy to think that God loved Esther more than Rahab or that He could've used Mary more than the woman at the well, God's love is not like ours. His love is never based on what we have or have not done. Author and speaker Beth Moore says, "When He who was, who is, and who is to come sees each of us, He sees who we were, who we are, and who we will become."[9]

When God saw Rahab, He didn't just see the city prostitute; He saw a scarlet cord of redemption, victory for the people of Israel, and a place in the lineage of Jesus. That dry, dusty day at the well, Jesus didn't just see a woman trying to find satisfaction in relationships with men. Jesus saw a new fountain of living water springing up in her life; He saw a town hearing the gospel and tasting of this well that never runs dry. God takes these women who have been defined by a past of sexual sin and says, "You are forgiven. Go and sin no more."[10]

We are all guilty of not following God's design for sex. We all struggle pursuing sexual wholeness. Know that who you were and who you are is not who you have to be. If you are God's daughter, you can walk changed in the freedom of obedience and forgiveness. Beth Moore encourages, "God can change what people do. He can change behavioral patterns that have been in play for decades. He can change what we do to cope, to find comfort, to survive conflict, to count. Like me, Rahab had done a same old thing for years … and then she did something new. She believed God and acted on it."[11]

Believe God when He says you are forgiven. If you are His own, whatever happened before today is washed by the blood of Jesus. He removes our filthy rags and clothes us with His robes of purity. Walk forth in freedom and in obedience, Sisters.

Commitment

When you continue to seriously date someone, you start (or should start) to consider marriage and life-long commitment. Commitment is a huge struggle among millennials (of which group I am a part). We are flaky. When the going gets tough, *we* get going. If we don't *feel* like it, we don't do it. So what's the big deal about commitment? Is it only important in a relationship?

Jamal Miller gave great insight regarding commitment:

It shows signs of your maturity in God, but it also shows signs of your maturity in your preparation for marriage. The number one challenge in your marriage is your ability to commit. Before you commit to a spouse, you should be committing to friends, to yourself, to church, to God. If you're having a hard time committing to God Who is perfect, Who is never going to hurt you, Who is never going to fail you, Who is never going to throw a shoe at you when He's mad, how will you ever be able to commit to someone who is imperfect?[12]

Before considering a relationship, look at the commitment in your own life first. Can you commit to a weekly Bible study? To attend church each week? To time with God in the morning? To a consistent workout routine and healthy eating? To a job? To a friend going through a tough time? To demanding family members? To responsibilities despite being tired, busy, unmotivated, or distracted? These areas in your life can show signs of your maturity in commitment and also in your preparation for marriage.

If you find yourself to be a woman of commitment, it can be difficult to find a man of commitment. The enemy is attacking commitment *before* marriage and commitment *after* marriage, so it is important to find a man who will remain faithful no matter what. One sign of his dedication is to look at the current obligations in all aspects of his life to see if he is loyal to his responsibilities.

Truly, we all have areas of commitment in which to grow, and dating can reveal your weaknesses in a convicting and challenging way. For example, you might be very committed to working out and eating healthy while your boyfriend is not and is challenged by it. On the other hand, your boyfriend might be very dedicated to his friends (he'll drop anything to help them out) and to talking through his thoughts and struggles with a mentor. You see his maturity, and it challenges you to be more like Christ in those areas. You can learn from each other's areas of strong commitment. Ask God to help grow you in mature commitment in *all* areas of your life. And look for a godly man who is maturing in his dedication as well.

Dating

Dating can be a difficult season to navigate within your singleness. It is not always as easy as they make it seem in the movies. Expect that there will be frustrations, learning curves, memories, tears, laughter, heartbreak, confusion, fun, lack of clarity, gain, loss, and everything in between. Keep Christ as your Rock. With Him, you will not be easily shaken.

SCENE 7

When Her Script Is What I Want

My childhood best friend and her college sweetheart are celebrating their fifth anniversary. Cool. Scroll. *Oh, look! Baby number three is on the way. Great.* Scroll. *Her wedding photos look amazing. They look like a model couple. I guess you only get a guy who looks like him if you look like she does.* Scroll. *Another vacation? This time it's Italy? The closest I'm getting to Italy right now is this pizza I'm eating.* Scroll. *SHE got engaged?!? Didn't I babysit her at some point? Oh my goodness! I feel like a grandma.* Scroll.

Comparison Is a Bad Travel Companion

Everyone is living their best life . . . except for me. I'm stuck in this season of singleness. These thoughts often creep into our minds when we go to social media and allow Instagram to interpret our script. Okay, so Instagram isn't the culprit. It is just a revealer of our hearts. Truly, we don't even need to get on our phones to fuel the feeling of "everyone but me." It's the TV show where people live in perfect houses and their conflicts are what they should wear and who didn't accept their party invite. It's the movie with the perfect happy ending. Goodness! It's even at church where you see that cute couple headed to the mission field together. Comparison is wherever we allow it to go.

I was flying out of the Nashville airport recently when I saw a big-time country music star, her NFL husband, and adorable kids at the ticket counter ahead of me. The family was perfect. Her hair was perfect. *She* was perfect. Several minutes later, I found myself walking down the terminal thinking about all the ways I did not measure up to her. Well, goodness . . . if that didn't just stop the joy and gratitude of the moment! This is *my* script that God has written for me. Who am I to be ungrateful? Comparison wanted to fly with me that day; but I really didn't want to get it at baggage claim, so I left it right then and there. I'm surprised it didn't set off the alarm at the security check.

Teddy Roosevelt famously and wisely said, "Comparison is the thief of joy." How true this is! I can have my joy stolen in one minute of scrolling, in one scene in a movie, in one character on a show, and in one line at the airport all because I allow comparison to quietly and slyly snuggle up next to me. Don't let that companion travel with you. It'll take up more space in your mind and heart than you want it to.

What Is That to You?

I saw the comparison struggle recently while reading through the book of John. The resurrected Jesus is on the beach with Peter. Jesus has just asked Peter three times if he loves Him. Peter assuredly answers, "Lord, you know that I love you." Jesus tells him, "Feed my sheep." Right after this command, Jesus interestingly reveals a *spoiler alert* in Peter's life:

> "I assure you: When you were young, you would tie your belt and walk wherever you wanted. But when you grow old, you will stretch out your hands and someone else will tie you and carry you where you don't want to go." He said this to signify by what kind of death he would glorify God. After saying this, He told him, "Follow Me!" (John 21:18-19 HCSB).

Jesus discloses to Peter that he (Peter) will be martyred one day. Jesus then commands Peter to follow Him. Can you imagine being Peter in this moment? You've just been told that you will die for your faith. Many of us don't know what tomorrow holds, so to be told how your life is going to end would be shocking. What does Peter do?

> So Peter turned around and saw the disciple Jesus loved following them. That disciple was the one who had leaned back against Jesus at the supper and asked, "Lord, who is the one that's going to betray You?" When Peter saw him, he said to Jesus, "Lord — what about him?" "If I want him to remain until I come," Jesus answered, "what is that to you? As for you, follow Me" (John 21:20-22 HCSB).

Peter sees his fellow disciple and asks, "What about him? Is he going to die the same death? Is my story the same as his?" This is his initial reaction to Jesus' prophecy. But I love Jesus's response. He basically says, "If he lives until I return, why should that matter to you? How does his death affect how you die? All I want you to do is follow Me."

The same is true for you and me. Your best friend gets married. What is that to you and your singleness? Follow Jesus. You are the only single girl in your friend group or at church. What is that to you and how you are going to live your life? Follow Jesus.

The beauty of reading this passage is knowing how the stories of Peter and John (the disciple Jesus loved) end. According to church history, Peter was crucified upside down, and John lived to an old age and died of natural causes. Their deaths were different and so were their life scripts. The closing scenes in their plays were drastically different. We could look at each of their final acts and classify one as a horror ending and the other as a simple drama. However, the beautiful and most important thing is that God used them both in great ways. One script was not better than the other. They both lived their lives in a God-honoring way and died in a way specific to God's unique plan for them.

We can all identify with Peter, especially if it seems as if our friends are getting married one by one. "What about her? What about me?" We start looking around and comparing, pointing fingers, and asking questions. What is that to you? Look up, not around, and follow Jesus.

Throw a Party

The Prodigal Son is another Bible story that shows our inclination toward comparison. When we read the story of the Prodigal Son, we tend to focus on the younger brother's rebellion and return. But the response of the older brother also has a message. Look at the passage, starting with the celebration the father throws for the younger brother's return.

> . . . So they began to celebrate. Now his older son was in the field; as he came near the house, he heard music and dancing. So he summoned one of the servants

and asked what these things meant. 'Your brother is here,' he told him, 'and your father has slaughtered the fattened calf because he has him back safe and sound.' Then he became angry and didn't want to go in (Luke 15:24b-28a HCSB).

How many times in my singleness do I respond like he did? I begrudge the fact that while I have been living a life dedicated to the Father, another sister of mine gets the celebration I have been wanting . . . a wedding, an anniversary, a baby shower, the job promotion. "Where is my celebration? I deserve it more than she deserves it."

The older brother unfortunately misses out on the celebration and fun because of his jealousy. Author and speaker Annie Downs once challenged her "older brother" self. "I can either help throw the party, or I can leave the party."[1] What a powerful message. How many times do I leave the party? I resent my Father because someone else is getting what I have been praying for. My sister is being celebrated. My Father is putting the robe on my sibling, and I am sulking. The Father invites me in, yet I turn away with bitter envy because the celebration does not center on me.

When you see the fatted calf killed for your restored sister, when you hear the music and dancing of a friend's joyful heart, when the Father gives her the gold ring, will you help throw the party or will you leave the party? Choose to enjoy the Father's presence and always rejoice when another sister is celebrated by Him.

Be a Happy Hostess

Let's look a little more into the concept of throwing a party. When throwing a party for someone else, be a happy hostess. Do not allow yourself to become someone who cannot attend weddings or who begrudges the engaged friend or who drops the friend who starts dating. Withholding joy for others is jealousy and is wrong. Romans 12:15a commands us to "rejoice with those who rejoice" (ESV).

It can seem easier to weep with friends when they are weeping. Our compassionate hearts are quick to put arms around hurting friends and lean in with listening ears. Rejoicing can be another thing. Jealousy creeps in and hinders true happiness for a sister-in-Christ. The desire to celebrate is there but so is the desire for what she has. It can be hard to lay your wants aside and celebrate with others.

In seasons of engagements, save-the-dates, wedding showers, gender reveal parties, and more, it can be easy to become bitter against God and withhold joy and celebration from our sisters. Don't allow the enemy to steal this joy. God has a unique script for each of His daughters. Choose to see His goodness and kindness to you and to your sisters . . . and then celebrate!

Realize Your Greatest Need Is the Father

Sometimes, like the older brother, I forget that I have the Father. I am with the Father Who sent His Son as a man, destined to die for me, to spare me from an eternity of separation and wrath. My greatest need is not having a reason to celebrate or having what she has. My greatest need is Him.

C.J. Mahaney expounds upon this by reminding us,

> Your greatest need is not a spouse. Your greatest need is to be delivered from the wrath of God — and that has already been accomplished for you through the death and resurrection of Christ. So why doubt that God will provide a much, much lesser need? Trust His sovereignty, trust His wisdom, trust His love.[2]

I forget that He takes great delight in me and rejoices over me with singing (Zephaniah 3:17). I don't remember that "every generous act and every perfect gift is from above" (James 1:17a HCSB). I forget that when I seek Him, I "will not lack any good thing" (Psalm 34:10). I get focused on what I want and on what God isn't giving me. I look around at others' seemingly perfect timing and compare it to my waiting. When I realize that deliverance from wrath is all I need — and that's already been provided by Jesus — I can be thankful for the gifts surrounding me. They are just added blessings. Remember what God has done for you. Trust that He will continue to do for you as He has done in the past. Reflect on His goodness and love. Focus on God Himself and not His gifts or the timing of His gifts.

Each Story Is Different

Peter, the older brother, you, and I all need to hear this reminder, My story is *not* your story. My story is not her story. My story is not anyone else's story — it is *mine*. Okay. Let's all say that truth five times slowly.

In reality, we will hear the stories of others. They surround us. They are the stories of our aunts and uncles. They are the accounts of Ruth and Boaz and Isaac and Rebekah. They are the stories of our friends. So how can we best respond?

Hope in Love Stories

I love to hear stories of how people met. I mean, who doesn't enjoy a good love story? Each story is different, unique, and an example of divine intervention regardless of how much romance, humor, or wrestling is involved. Here are a few of my favorite love stories.

A hitchhiker was looking for a ride back to college when another man about his age pulled over and offered a ride. "I'm stopping by my girlfriend's house, though, before I head that direction. She does have a younger sister, so it might be worth your time." The hitchhiker was my grand-father. He married the younger sister who became my grandmother. The man offering the ride married his girl-friend, and they became my great-uncle and great-aunt. An unexpected, adventurous love story.

My great-grandmother Viola lived in Georgia. She was unmarried and in her early 20s. In that era, she was considered an old maid. Unbeknownst to her, her two married sisters placed a singles ad with her information in a national magazine. A man named Richard from Davenport, Iowa, started writing to her. This was a dilemma in that era as she was the granddaughter of a Confederate soldier, and he was the grandson of a Union officer. The realities and emotions of the Civil War were still looming. However, letters continued to be delivered by the postman. Richard took a train to Georgia with the hope of being welcomed by an understanding father and not the barrel of a shotgun. He and Viola were soon married. A culture-defying love story.

My parents were set up on a blind date and fell in love at first sight. They both knew on that date that they were supposed to marry one another. My dad said to my mom, (Can we talk about how this was their first date?) "I'm going on my honeymoon to the Bahamas in August. Want to go with me?" This was in January. My mom, coy and with a sparkle in her eyes replied, "I'll have to see about that." They got engaged in April, married in August, and, sure enough, set off on their honeymoon to the Bahamas that same month. A whirlwind romance.

My good friend knew she was supposed to marry her now husband. But she fought it all along because he wasn't what she expected (looks, age, personality, family, etc.). Even on her wedding day, she wrestled — not so much because of him but because she knew her selfish sin nature and what marriage would require of her. However, she knew that she loved him and that his love for her was constant despite her doubts. She knew that it was what God had for her, and she thanks God every day that she chose him over her faulty and flaky emotions. A glorious struggle of love.

But as much as I enjoy a good love story, especially these, I have to stop myself sometimes because I can start writing myself into someone else's story. *"Maybe it will happen to me like that? If I could just . . ."* And then I dream of manipulating circumstances so my story will turn out just as funny or romantic as the next. It can be easy in singleness to cling to the hope found in the stories of others. But God does not want us to try to control our stories. He wants us to trust Him to work things out in His timing and in His way.

Hopeless in Love Stories

We love what we hear in others' stories, so we make adjustments accordingly so our stories can turn out like theirs. "She found someone when she was working with the teen group at church. Maybe if I start serving there, then I will find someone too." But then we end up manipulating people and circumstances and our motivation to serve is wrong.

"She was ____ years old when she got married, and I'm ____ years old. My situation is hopeless!" We read each other's love stories as a formula; and if one part of the formula is off for us, then we think God is not capable of writing us a beautiful story. I am reminded of Hebrews 12:1. "Therefore, since we are surrounded by so great a cloud of witnesses, let us also lay aside every weight, and sin which clings so closely, and let us run with endurance the race that is set before us" (ESV). We often find ourselves trying to run the race of the girl beside us. We want her race and not our own. We have the cloud of witnesses surrounding us — those who have gone before us. But the Lord is not asking us or wanting us to replicate those stories. Instead, He wants us to see the faith of other believers and ultimately to see the faithfulness of God. Don't cling to the stories of others; rather, be encouraged by their trust in God and in how God showed His kindness to them. Then run the race set before you; live the story being written. It is going to be good.

Hope in Love Himself

God does not want you to try to create a story that is not your own. Another person's story is not your hope; Jesus should be your greatest hope. Jesus cares for you and knows your needs. Put hope in the story of love that your Savior is writing for you.

The beautiful love story written for me: God saw me — His beautiful daughter, fearfully and wonderfully made. But I didn't see God. My heart was full of selfish ambition, pride, hatred, and enmity toward God. I was headed the opposite direction, away from Him. He asked too much of me. He wanted me to admit that I wasn't enough and that I needed Him. I felt that, as an independent woman, I could fend for myself. But as I headed down my own path, I kept hearing His woos of affection for me. I saw His acts of selfless love. I read of His death and resurrection, completed because He wanted me to be with Him forever. He pursued me despite my lack of interest. And then my heart started to change. I felt new life bubbling from within me. I was giddy with joy. And then I said YES to the Lover of my soul. A life-long, death-will-never-do-us-part marriage. What a story! There is no greater love story. There is no greater surprise or unexpected twist in the plot than the one being written for us.

Whether I find the man of my dreams and have a cute *You've Got Mail* type story, I meet a man in a boring-not-too-exciting way, or I never end up marrying at all, I know that I am not living for the thrill of a love story made in this world. I am living for the joy of the otherworldly one. The story of how I met my First Love is one that I will be telling for years to come.

SCENE 8

She Spoke into My Script

Words can either nourish or drain. As Christians, we are called to edify and lift each other up. But how do you encourage a friend when you don't understand her season? How do you know if your words are nourishing or draining? Many married women desire to know how to best encourage a single sister-in-Christ. What to say. What not to say. Also, sometimes it can be hard to receive encouragement as a single woman from a woman who, perhaps in our minds, has what we want. We think, "Of course, it is easy for you to say that. You are not where I am. You are on the other side of the difficulty. You have never experienced this season like I have."

Conversation between married and single women becomes like the game of telephone: one person whispers something into another person's ear, and then that person whispers what they heard in the next person's ear until you get to the end, and the message is completely different. The intention of the message from the married sister-in-Christ is good but can get twisted by the Enemy and come across as something totally different when it reaches the ears and heart of her single friend. How can we better understand each other and communicate more clearly the message of encouragement? It takes two to communicate.

Single Sisters Receiving Encouragement

It can be hard to receive encouragement or rebuke from someone not in the same season of life. Sometimes I want a friend in another season to speak into my situation because I just want to cling to the hopeful words of "It's going to be okay" or "It turned out for me so it will turn out well for you, too." But most of the time I think "they have no idea what I'm going through" and push their words aside. I have missed out on a lot of godly wisdom because of this attitude. We cannot negate someone's encouragement just because they lack the experience of the situation. God does not add qualifiers to speaking into the lives of each other. "Therefore encourage one another and build each other up *only if you are in the same season of life.*" No. The Bible says it plainly in I Thessalonians 5:11. "Therefore encourage one another and build each other up as you are already doing" (HCSB). The Bible does not have an age, season, degree, or status qualifier for who can encourage.

When being encouraged, it is important to humbly receive the truth, to listen with purity of heart, and to extend grace.

Humbly receive the truth. In James 1:21b-22, we are commanded to "humbly receive the implanted word, which is able to save you. But be doers of the word and not hearers only, deceiving yourselves" (HCSB). If our sister is speaking truth to us — whether she is married, divorced, widowed, single, or dating — we need to listen in humility and then go and do.

Listen with purity of heart. If you love your brother- or sister-in-Christ, listen with love. Be patient, believing the best in all things, not getting easily angered, trusting, looking for the best, and rejoicing in truth.[1] Don't look for hidden motives. See their hearts to love you well, even if words fail. Take their words of encouragement as just that — encouragement. If they are admonishing you, have an open mind. Ask God to search your heart.

Extend grace. People may not say the right thing. In fact, they often don't. Their words may very well come across as hurtful. Rather than taking offense, consider — what are their intentions? What are they desiring to say? Then thank them for their love for you. If it seems beneficial, take it a step further and open up the conversation. "I really appreciate your words. I know you love me and want to speak into my life. It can be hard to know exactly what people need in different situations. Right now, I really need to hear you say _____." Be honest and communicate your needs. Then you can both grow in communication and in understanding of each other.

Married Sisters Giving Encouragement

Married sisters who are reading — listen up! Single women can be touchy when receiving words from married women. It's not the right response. But when marriage is a desire, it can be difficult for single women to hear words of encouragement and wisdom from married women. This should not, however, discourage married women from speaking into the lives of singles. We need married women and their words!

Above all, speak with love. I Corinthians 13:1 says, "If I speak human or angelic languages but do not have love, I am a sounding gong or a clanging cymbal" (HCSB). How many times have our words been loud and obnoxious? Guilty here! Remind your friend of your love for her.

Most of the time, a single woman just wants a listening ear. We want someone to acknowledge the difficulty of what we are going through. I am a listener; but as a Two on the Enneagram, I also really want to help people. If there is a problem, I want to fix it. I have come to realize that some problems were not meant to be fixed by me. Sometimes the best way I can help is to simply listen.

I remember the wake-up call I had recently with a friend who — *gasp* — didn't need my light-shining words of wisdom. What!? It was one of my close married friends who was going through the pain of infertility. God had been teaching me so much about trusting Him with my lack of a husband, and I wanted to encourage her to trust Him with her lack of a child. She looked at me square in the face. "Lauren. I know the truth. I know all the right answers. I'm trying to get my heart to trust those answers. I'm thankful for your words, but I just really need you to listen right now." It was a holy-hush of a moment. My friend needed a shoulder to cry on and a friend to say "I see your pain." Now, when a friend is confiding in me with her struggles, I pray for wisdom — wisdom to know if I need a holy hush or wisdom for words in my holy whispers.

Holy Whispers

When a single woman needs a holy whisper, what helps? Proverbs 15:23 says, "A man takes joy in giving an answer; and a timely word — how good that is!" (HCSB). I have had many timely words spoken to me when my heart was hungry for encouragement. Words can bring light into hard or misunderstood seasons. Being on the giving end, it can be hard to know what to say.

"I may not know the experience, but I know some of the same feelings." Many of my married friends have never experienced singleness as an adult. Most only have their experience of being single in college. Even if they have been single at some point, singleness looks different in your 20s, 30s, 40s, and beyond. Each season comes with different challenges. To say they know exactly what I'm currently experiencing may not be true. I do the same thing, though. I want to empathize with my friends. I want to connect with them. I want to be able to say, "I know what you are going through." However, most of the time I have never been in their shoes. Saying that I know how it feels when I don't can put up a wall and close up the receptiveness of their heart.

Going back to my conversation with my mentor Susanne on rejection, she gave me great clarity in navigating how to comfort a friend. She expressed empathy in a *similar emotion* rather than in a *similar experience*. She said, "I have never been rejected in this way, but I have felt rejection before. Even more so, Jesus has felt the feeling of rejection — for you." She had never been in my situation, but she could identify with the feeling. In addition, she connected the fact that Jesus had also been rejected.

She wanted to help me know that I was not alone in experiencing this feeling. Others have and will experience it, and there is great rejoicing in the fellowship of suffering. While our experiences are different, we have all felt discontented, alone, frustrated, annoyed, confused, angry, and fearful. Connect in those feelings.

"Regardless of what you are experiencing, it does not change who you are." Sometimes we can feel like a disappointment to our grandmothers or to our moms because we are not following in the footsteps of other family members who are married with five children. It can seem as if there is nothing going on in our lives because the answer to the sweet lady at church seems to never change. "Nope. Still nobody new in my life." We feel as if the world and the church culture are telling us we are behind on life or that something is wrong with us.

I am so thankful for the married people in my life who remind me of who God says I am and who they see me to be. "You are loved. You are valuable. You are strong and capable of so much. Your relationship status will never change who I see you to be." Those words are so refreshing to hear. Let us remind each other of these truths regardless of the season.

"I am here for you." We sometimes need a shoulder to cry on and a friend to laugh with. We want a listening ear, and

we long to know that no matter what happens, you will be there for us.

"I see you as more than your relationship status." Going to family gatherings or a church get-together as a single can feel as if we have a big red target over our heads. Show us you care by genuinely caring about what is going on in our lives. There is more to our life than just a relationship or the lack of a relationship. Ask about our jobs, hobbies, passions, dreams, opportunities, friends, vacations, plans, etc. We always have so much going on.

"God sees you right where you are." We need to be reminded that God loves us and has not forgotten about us. If marriage is a desire of ours that is seemingly nowhere on the horizon, it can feel as if God does not care about our dreams or does not see us. I think of Hagar, left out in the wilderness, mistreated, ready to die. She felt alone and without purpose. But God saw her. He sent an Angel of the Lord to her to give her direction. Hagar responds beautifully in Genesis 16:13. "So she called the LORD who spoke to her: The God Who Sees, for she said, 'In this place, have I actually seen the One who sees me?'" (HCSB)

The same God who saw Hagar sees us. Married friends, remind your single friends of this truth. We can feel like Hagar out in the wilderness sometimes. Remind us that God sees us and has a beautiful plan for our lives. Then pray for us. Don't just pray that God will provide us with a husband; pray that God will help us grow in contentment and in the knowledge of Who He is.

"Want to hang out?" I have been a third wheel, a fifth wheel, and a ninth wheel so many times, but I still love it when my married friends ask me to hang out with them. I was invited to a game night one time where we competed guys against girls. There were three couples and then me. I was the odd man out, but we made do. It ended up being a fun night. It was nice to be included and asked to hang out — not because I had a husband to ensure even-numbered teams, but because my friend enjoys my company and wanted me to come. Married friends, don't forget your single friends. Ask us to hang out.

Holy Hushes

Each person is different. Some things may bother certain people more than others. But there are many common phrases said by well-meaning people that can feel like a stab in the heart. Just as the right words spoken at the right time can be incredibly encouraging, the wrong words spoken at the wrong time can be incredibly discouraging. Stop and think before you let these questions or statements cross your lips to your single friends.

"Why are you still single?" And to that we say — "Good question. I'll let you know when I figure it out." This question hurts and causes us to feel as if something is wrong

with us. A relationship status can't necessarily be controlled, and it is frustrating to be asked a question about something I feel as if I can do nothing about.

"Be thankful that you're single. Marriage is so much harder." Our minds go to those Friday nights spent alone at home when we wish we had someone beside us. Or the hesitancy to purchase those plane tickets across the sea because it is not as much fun to experience it alone. We know marriage is hard, but singleness is hard too. The Body of Christ does not need a "my horse is bigger than your horse" challenge on the difficulties of different seasons.

"You'll find someone one day. Your time is coming. You'll be next." Marriage is not promised at all in the Bible. We have no guarantee that every believer will be married. In fact, Paul urges believers to remain single if at all possible. Don't give false hope that a husband will come along because what if he doesn't? Thinking that God did not deliver on something (that He never even promised in the first place) will cause deep bitterness and resentment.

"When you fix your eyes on Jesus, your man will come along at the right time." Encourage us to pursue Christ alone and not Christ plus getting a man too. When given this formula, it is easy to think that serving Jesus equals getting what you want. That is the Prosperity Gospel and is not biblical. Sometimes God is gracious and shows extravagant grace by giving us something we don't deserve when

we aren't even following after Him. The Christian walk is not a formula used to get what we want. Many individuals quote Psalm 37:4 which says, "Delight yourself in the LORD, and he will give you the desires of your heart" (ESV). But when we delight ourselves in God, He starts molding us to be more like Jesus, and our hearts start to change to reflect His. He renews our hearts and our desires to be according to His will. God longs for us to pursue Him because we love Him, not with an ulterior motive of getting what we want.

There are many more things whispered that would be better off as a holy hush. There are also many hushes that need a holy whisper. It goes back to communication — married sisters, ask your single friend, "What helps? What doesn't help?" The conversation and the genuine interest to encourage will provide a beautiful bond.

Common Ground

If we are in different seasons of life, then we have nothing in common. This is a prevalent lie among women within the church. A single woman sees a married woman and thinks their walks share nothing. A young mom sees a widow and finds no similarities in their lives. A mom of many children feels no place to interact with a woman fighting infertility.

Different seasons and different pain means nothing in common, right? This could not be further from the truth.

If we are in Christ, we share identities. We are the daughters of the King, holy, chosen, set-apart, dearly loved, and called for a purpose. As previously mentioned, we share similar emotions. We experience loneliness, insecurity, inadequacy, anger, frustration, impatience, doubt, etc. The way these struggles surface may vary due to our differing circumstances, but we can still connect and encourage one another.

Jenilyn Swett, a single woman, shared a personal example in a *Christianity Today* article. "I have seen God work in some very particular ways in my relationships with married women who are struggling with infertility . . . The longing to be married and the longing for a healthy pregnancy are similar. Both are upheld but not guaranteed in Scripture, both involve dealing with waiting, hope, and disappointment. Some of the women who have been most tender toward my singleness are those who have struggled at length with infertility."[2]

Sisters, seek to love each other with the confidence and knowledge that we have much in common despite our different seasons of life. Our community is vital to our walk and to our faith. We need each other. Open your hearts to receive wisdom from and to give wisdom to sisters in different seasons. Otherwise, you may never know the insight they have to offer. As always, cover your hearts and your words with grace and peace.

SCENE 9

The Troupe

"Don't do life alone." This is the theme that my church recently embraced, emphasizing the importance of community in the life of a believer, and let me tell you — it is true! A single girl can't live this life single-handedly.

The Church
Single Women Loving the Church

In the world, you may feel like you don't have a place. But in the Body of Christ, you are a vital member. You are part of the whole body which is fitted and knit together by *every* supporting ligament. The Body grows and builds itself up in love by the proper working of *each* individual part, and a healthy church uses all people in all seasons.

God specifically called you, in your season of singleness, to play a role in building up the Body of Christ, in unifying believers in faith, and in maturing your brothers and sisters in the knowledge of Jesus.[1]

Your church needs you.

And you need the church.

God uses your unique gifts to serve the Church. I see God working through my friend Elizabeth's life as she ministers to her high school girls. My friend Christina faithfully teaches preschoolers every Sunday morning. Sarah holds the door open and smiles as she greets those walking into church. We each play a part in the Body.

God uses the Church to cultivate community in your life. The Church provides opportunities to connect with women in both the same and different stages of life. Women in community help one another fight against feelings of loneliness. They use the truth to help us understand God and His purposes. Together we encourage and uplift each other as we walk the journey of faith.

As women in a season of singleness, we often find ourselves like little children tossed by the waves of the world and blown around by every wind of lies and deceit. At church we find truth spoken in love. As believers, our goal isn't marriage — our goal is to become more like Christ. God looks at His Church and sees His children, free from categorization. Galatians 3:27-28 says, "For as many of you as have been baptized into Christ have put on Christ like a garment. There is no Jew or Greek, slave or free, male or female; for you are all one in Christ Jesus" (HCSB). In the Church, neither you nor the woman next to you is defined as single or married. You are daughters of the King with equal access to the throne of grace, equal at the foot of the Cross. What comfort and freedom!

When Church Hurts

Despite how the Bible says the Church should be, it is not what it should be. We live in a broken world. The Church is made up of imperfect people, and because of that, sometimes it hurts to go to church.

As a single, you look around and are surrounded by couples and families. You feel as if you are the only one walking into church without someone. It can feel lonely. Satan wants to magnify your loneliness and drown out the truth. I love how my friend Sarah decided to act against the lies of the enemy. She had started to feel the pain of attending church. It was hard knowing where to sit, and she felt out of place in a sea of people. She recognized that these struggles made her want to skip church because she didn't enjoy the reminders of not belonging. It can be so much easier to just sit at home and watch online, right? But Sarah knew herself well enough to know that if she didn't have purpose or accountability, then she would continue to sit on her couch on Sunday mornings and miss out on the fellowship and community she desperately needed. So she volunteered to start serving. She knew that if she were on the schedule to serve, then she would be there. She saw serving as getting the focus off of herself and her problems and putting the focus on others.

When Sarah shared this in our small group, several of the other girls admitted that they also felt the same way. They hated sitting by themselves, so we started texting each other in our group chat before church. "Hey I'm going to the 9:40 service. Anyone else?" Now we meet up, sit together, and sometimes do lunch. These girls did not allow the hurt of going to church alone to stop them from being in community and from worshipping our God.

The struggle of getting to church and finding a place to sit is one thing. But what about once you get there and have to talk to people? The things people do or don't say. The endless questions. The pity. The inability to connect because singleness feels like a disease. Don't allow these hurts to keep you from having community with people. Sometimes people don't understand singleness, and they don't always know how to connect. They only see life from their experiences. Instead of keeping to yourself or avoiding certain people, choose to see these instances as perfect opportunities to extend grace. These dear brothers- and sisters-in-Christ may always miss seeing and understanding the freedom and beauty of your season if you don't take the time and grace to help them see and understand. Instead of using these struggles as an excuse, see them as opportunities to share what God is doing in your life and how God is using your singleness for His glory.

What is your church struggle? How can you overcome that struggle? Don't let these hurts, pains, and awkward situations deter you from being obedient to God and faithfully attending a local body of believers.

The Church Loving Single Women

If you are married or have a platform in the church, here are some ideas on how you can love the single women in your church:

Don't promote messages of "waiting for a man" as if completeness is found in a husband.

Don't talk just about marriage and family. Acknowledge us and our struggles in sermon examples, illustrations, Bible study topics, and conversations. Sometimes we are led to feel as if we are behind in life.

Don't promote marriage as the end goal. Christ is the goal. Don't talk as if marriage is promised to us. Instead, remind us of Jesus' promise that He will never leave us or forsake us.

Don't emphasize our singleness or dating lives. We have other things happening in our lives. We don't want to always be reminded of our singleness. Ask about our passions, goals, professional lives, gifts, or service.

Do change the conversation and reactions about our singleness. We don't want to feel pity or less important because we haven't been chosen as wives yet.

Do find a place for us at church and make us feel welcome. Invite us to sit with you. Talk to us.

Do open your homes and families for us. We want to feel a part of something.

Do invest in us and pour into us. We want to be loved and nurtured.

Do celebrate our season like Paul celebrates it. Paul tries to convince people to stay single. Study and see the values he sees in it.

Do love us and let us know you need us.

You need us. And we need you.

Small Group
Women Intentionally Doing Life Together

Small group. Discipleship group. Community group. Bible study group. Whatever you or your church call it, you need to be a part of one.

I lead a small group at my house on Tuesday nights for other young professional women my age. Each week we gather around the table for food and laughter. Then we fill our coffee cups and head to the couches to open up our hearts and our Bibles. God has moved in big ways. He has moved in small ways. But, oh! How He has moved!

The beautiful thing about this community of women that gathers each week is that over the past three years of meeting, we have been able to watch each other grow in our love for Jesus and to see Him guide us along the journey. We have been there for each other during break-ups, grad school, turning in resignation letters, searching for new jobs, good days, bad days, prayer requests, praises, weddings, tears, laughter, etc. And we can say "Remember how God provided last time for you? Well, He is going to do it again," or "Don't be discouraged! You've grown so much in Jesus. He is working in your life. You may not be able to see it, but we do." We know how to "stir one another to love and good works"[2] and how to encourage one another.

When I first moved to the Nashville area after college, I knew no one my age. I found making friends extremely difficult since I was working full time and wasn't from the area. Being unmarried, I craved community and struggled with loneliness. At church, I didn't really fit into the college group, and I certainly wasn't a part of the young marrieds, so I searched for a small group and found one for young professional single women.

It changed my life.

I found godly friends. I learned honesty and vulnerability. I was challenged in my faith. My singleness took on meaning and purpose. I was a part of this group for two-and-a-half years before we had to disband due to family responsibilities of the leader. So I started the small group in my home, and the life changing impact continued. We are not meant to do life alone. God's intent is for us to encourage each other to be more like Jesus and to hold to His truth. Jesus had twelve men with whom He did life, and I believe He intended to model community and discipleship for His followers.

What does the Bible say about gathering together? Matthew 18:20 says that when there are two or three gathered in Jesus' name, He is in the midst. What a beautiful place to bring prayer requests. Galatians 6:2 calls us to bear one another's burdens. We help make each other's loads light. Proverbs 27:17 encourages us to sharpen and strengthen each other. I can use my strengths to help my sister with her weakness; she can use her gifts to encourage me in my walk. James 5:16 commands us to confess our sins to each other. Our sins can weigh us down and make us spiritually and even physically sick. Confession and admittance can restore our weary souls. 2 Timothy 3:16-17 reminds us of the power that comes from studying God's Word together. The Bible equips us, teaches us, corrects us, trains us, and readies us for the Christian walk. Hebrews 3:13 warns us that if we aren't exhorting one another, we can become hardened by sin. What holy work we can do if we make time and space in our schedules to gather together![3]

Hospitable Community
Social Hostility versus Social Hospitality

Whether you are single or you are reading this book to gain a better understanding of singles, be a safe place for those unmarried in your life by practicing social hospitality. Your presence should offer safety and refuge in group settings. It can be dangerously easy to see other single women as competition for attention and create an environment of social hostility. As women, we like to make ourselves look better than other women and don't like to allow our "competition" to feel at ease or comfortable. You know what I'm talking about. It can be a dog-eat-dog world out there among us women. We snub others in an attempt to make ourselves feel better and to assuage the insecurities we carry. We ignore those who have nothing to offer us. Single women view other single women as rivals. But this is not how we are called to treat image bearers. Each person is precious in God's sight and deserves respect, love, and surroundings of social hospitality rather than social hostility.

Let me give you an example of social hostility versus social hospitality by explaining the feelings I felt at two weddings I attended recently (both without a Plus One). The first wedding did not feel like a safe place socially for me. I experienced social hostility. I saw several people I had not seen in a few years, and it was so good to see them and catch up. Also in attendance was another single girl with whom I share several mutual friends and whom I was eager to meet since I had heard so much about her. She was cordial at first. But as the evening went on, I was left out of the group. I felt "less than" and not accepted. She didn't include me in any conversation, and her body language conveyed a lack of interest in getting to know me and in letting me in on her fun that evening. I felt as if I were in a competition — a competition for which I did not sign up to participate. (These were *feelings*, and I could be completely misinterpreting them. Regardless, when I got home, I had to process these feelings and remind myself of the truth.)

Experiencing this social hostility spurred me on to extend social hospitality at my next opportunity. Literally, the next day I attended another wedding where I sat with two of my single friends and a married couple. I spotted another single girl whom I had not seen in awhile and whom I really didn't know well. I could tell she came by herself. Feelings from the wedding the night before flooded back, and I knew I had the power to create either social hostility or social hospitality for this girl. So I hugged her, saved her a place at our table, and welcomed her into the conversation for the afternoon.

Hospitality is not just inviting someone into your house to have a meal. Hospitality can be inviting someone in with your presence, kindness, and warmth. Hospitality is defined as "the friendly reception and treatment of guests or strangers."[4] When you interact with others, are you hospitable? Do you make them feel loved and valued? Philippians 2:3 reminds us to "Do nothing from selfish ambition or conceit, but in humility count others more significant than yourselves" (ESV). No matter with whom you interact — single, married, popular, unpopular — treat them as more important than yourself. Don't use people to your advantage. Imagine yourself in their shoes. How would you want to feel? The next verse continues the challenge. "Let each of you look not only to his own interests, but also to the interests of others" (Philippians 2:4 ESV). Be on the lookout! When you are in social settings, look for other women by themselves who may need social hospitality. Is there a mom sitting by herself in front of you at church? Invite her to sit with you — or go sit with her! What about that single girl who isn't quite sure where to sit at the wedding? Ask her to join your conversation!

Hebrews 13:1-2a says, "Let brotherly [or sisterly] love continue. Do not neglect to show hospitality to strangers" (ESV).

Don't Do Life Alone

If you are not attending a Bible-believing church, step into obedience this week and start attending this Sunday. If you are not in a small community of people who know you, love you, support you, and speak truth to you, find one. Ask your church for possible groups, search for Bible studies near you, or, better yet, start one. In a social setting? Avoid social hostility and extend social hospitality.

God never intended us to do this single life alone.

ACT III

The Author

SCENE 10
Unknown Endings

What if it never happens? What if I never get married? These questions can be haunting. The fear of the unknown or the potential answer of "never" can rattle you. Other times it seems okay not to have an answer, and it's simply a matter of trusting. But the truth is, the answer *cannot* be known right now.

The Worry of Tomorrow

Jesus knew that there would be things in all of our lives that we would long to know and about which we would worry. In His Sermon on the Mount in Matthew, Jesus lovingly speaks to the crowd and to us.

135

This is why I tell you: *Don't worry about your life,* what you will eat or what you will drink; or about your body, what you will wear. Isn't life more than food and the body more than clothing? Look at the birds of the sky: They don't sow or reap or gather into barns, yet your heavenly Father feeds them. Aren't you worth more than they? Can any of you add a single cubit to his height by worrying? And why do you worry about clothes? Learn how the wildflowers of the field grow: they don't labor or spin thread. Yet I tell you that not even Solomon in all his splendor was adorned like one of these! If that's how God clothes the grass of the field, which is here today and thrown into the furnace tomorrow, *won't He do much more for you—you of little faith?* So don't worry, saying, "What will we eat?" or "What will we drink?" or "What will we wear?" For the idolaters eagerly seek all these things, and your heavenly Father knows that you need them. But *seek first the kingdom of God and His righteousness,* and all these things will be provided for you. *Therefore don't worry about tomorrow, because tomorrow will worry about itself. Each day has enough trouble of its own"* (Matthew 6:25-34 HCSB, emphasis added).

Jesus commands the crowd *not* to worry about tomorrow. What good does worry do? It only stresses you and makes you miss out on the opportunities that God has for you right now. Life is more than food, clothing, your body, your relationship status. Our purpose for life is glorifying God. Will that be through marriage? Maybe. Will that be through singleness? We know for sure right now that answer is yes. Maybe you need a picture of a wildflower or a vase of some beautiful wildflowers on those difficult days to remind you that God takes care of the wildflowers and clothes them in such beautiful ways. How much more is He going to take care of you? He knows your desires. He knows your needs — even more than you know them. *Do you believe this? Do you trust this?*

Speak Truth to Yourself

So when I'm tempted to worry and stress out about what tomorrow, next year, or the next ten years look like, I can say to myself, "My heavenly Father knows what I need. I am to seek first the kingdom of God and His righteousness, and all the things I need will be provided for me." Write it. Say it out loud. Believe it. Remember — "Stop *listening* to yourself and start *talking* to yourself." It is easy to listen to our emotions too much. We need to start talking to them and telling them the truth that God has spoken to us. Let's get a handle on the emotional rollercoasters filled with the nauseating ups and downs of lies!

Focus on Today

How are you being beautifully clothed today? How has God provided for you this week? Look at the blessings around you. I know a girl who really struggled in her singleness. All she wanted was to be married. She complained and whined about how awful singleness was and talked about how all her friends were married. Then, one day, she met someone and eventually got married. I was overjoyed for her! A year or so in, all she could focus on was not having a baby and how all of her friends had a baby. The root of her struggle wasn't being single or being childless — it was discontentment. Is this you? Do you see the blessings around you no matter what season of life you are in? Are you focused on what you *do* have or what you *do not* have? Focusing on the beautiful clothing with which God has adorned us takes daily practice, meditation on truth, and prayer. It is a learned behavior and a Spirit-led response.

Seek the Kingdom of God

Are you busy doing God's work? Truly seek — search, be on the lookout, hunt, try to find — the kingdom of God around you. Where is He leading you to use your gifts? When you are in quest of what God is doing around you and through you, you are focused on the here and now. You will still have struggles and difficulties, but they will be seen with a heavenly perspective.

Unfulfilled Desires

Does God give us desires He may never fulfill? I wonder about this all the time, and I don't have pretty, clear-cut answers. So I cling to what I do know and remind myself of those things.

God's Character: He is kind and loves me so much.

God's Timing: Many people in the Bible had longings; they prayed for children, for deliverance, for entrance to the Promised Land, for the coming of a Deliverer, etc. In many cases, according to His perfect timing, God answered yes. God wrote them each a beautiful story.

God's Bigger Picture. Sometimes these desires are fulfilled unexpectedly or in a different way than we could foresee.

God's Child: He gave me His Son. Therefore, He will not withhold anything good from me. Psalm 84:11 says, "For the LORD God is a sun and shield; the LORD bestows favor and honor. No good thing does he withhold from those who walk uprightly" (ESV).

God's Heavenly Kingdom: Our desires and longings have deeper meaning. They point toward our longings for heaven where all will be made right.

God's Incomprehensibility: I don't understand God. His ways are higher than mine. But I can trust Him.

Even If You Don't

The real question is *what will you do with God if He never provides a husband for you?* I am reminded of a recent conversation I had with a coworker who described a difficult situation. He prayed for God to take the situation away, but God did not. As a result, my coworker turned away from God. He wanted nothing to do with Him. Is God only good if your circumstances are good? According to the Bible, He is a kind Father. He knows what good gifts to give us. Do you trust this when hard things happen in your life?

I am reminded of the beautiful words that MercyMe sings:

> "It's easy to sing when there's nothing to bring me down. But what will I say when I'm held to the flame like I am right now? . . . I know You're able and I know you can save through the fire with your mighty hand . . . I know the sorrow, and I know the hurt would all go away if You'd just say the word but *even if You don't, my hope is You alone.*"[1]

My hope is God and God alone. My hope is *not* in marriage, in a man, in a feeling of love. My hope is in the unchangeable, almighty God.

Wrestle with the question "What if I never get married?" Will you be bitter against God? Will you turn away from Him? Will your lack of a husband consume the fullness that God offers? You need to come to an *"even if you don't"* statement with God. Write out the desires of your heart and then answer them with an *"even if you don't"* heart response.

I desire to be married, but *even if you don't* provide me with a husband, I will still love you and serve you with joy. I will devote myself to you with the same devotion I desire to give to my husband.

I desire to have children, but *even if you don't* bless me with physical children, I will find and mentor spiritual children and hold them up in thanks.

I desire _____, *but even if you don't* _____ .

Life will be filled with *even if you don'ts*. It's how you handle them that will reveal your faith and determine your steps.

God Is Not Defined by Circumstances

Our circumstances don't define God. They may reveal something about God, but they don't define Him. We have to go to His Word to find interpretations for our circumstances.

The Lord has a sovereign plan for my life. I may not understand it. I may wish it looked different. But His ways are so much better than mine! How can I even determine or judge God's ways? He is the Creator. He is all-wise. I must trust in Him and in His Word. Romans 11:33-34 says, "Oh, the depth of the riches and the wisdom and knowledge of God! How unsearchable are his judgments and how inscrutable his ways! 'For who has known the mind of the Lord, or who has been his counselor?'" (ESV). It is impossible to understand or interpret all of God's ways. They are unexplainable, unfathomable, and mysterious. Who am I to demand my way from this richly wise God? One commentary adds that "His wisdom and His ways are higher than ours. He is not a God whom we can neatly define or easily explain, and the things that He does reveal to us often leave us speechless."[2]

This reminds me of God's urging in my life to write this book. I had just been rejected by a guy and was feeling utterly lost and confused. I had really hoped that he was the one for me. I had no plans of returning to singleness. So I prayed. Over and over again, I begged God to speak truth and direction to me. "Lord, please speak to me." Well, He did. I was really hoping He would tell me to be patient because this guy would call, apologize, and want to get back together. I also pondered that maybe God would comfort me in the fact that someone better was just around the corner.

Instead, He spoke another word that definitely left me speechless. I was sitting on my couch one morning, praying again, "Lord, please speak to me!" His presence overwhelmed me and His Word penetrated my heart. "I'm not done with your singleness yet." *What*!? Surely I did not hear that correctly. But He spoke it again gently. "I'm not done with your singleness yet." This was not the word I was praying for or that I wanted to hear.

Later that week, I was at church, and the Lord spoke again, this time through the speaker and his message. The message was about following God's calling for your life. The speaker said something like this, "Some of you in this room have heard God speak to you, and you are too fearful to obey. When will you step into obedience and surrender?"

God spoke another time that week through a podcast message. (He definitely answered my prayers of speaking to me!) I finally lifted up my hands in surrender and yielded to His leading. I started praying, "Lord, what do you want me to do with my singleness?" That's when He spoke to me again and called me to write this book. Would I have chosen this path and written my story this way? Definitely not. However, His ways are higher than my ways. His plans are not my plans. And though the journey has been different than I would've dreamed, it has been beautiful.

Paul in Romans 11:35-36 continues, "'Or who has given a gift to him that he might be repaid?' For from him and through him and to him are all things. To him be glory forever. Amen" (ESV). It is true that "we deserve nothing from God except His wrath and can demand nothing from Him, neither mercy nor, even, answers. God is at the centre of His plans (v. 36). Contrary to our self-centred ideas, God's work does not revolve around us."[3] Not only are His plans above ours, but we must accept that we don't even deserve our definition of "good plans" since all we really deserve is wrath from God. God owes us nothing. Anything He bestows on us is due to His mercy and His grace. All that He gives us or doesn't give us is due to His glory and to making His name great.

Unfulfilled Longings for Motherhood
The past few Mother's Days have made me cry.

I remember Mother's Day at church a few years back when a lady came on stage to welcome guests. "Today may be hard for you if you've lost a mother, are estranged from your mother, lost a child that made you a mother, or want to be a mother but can't be due to physical difficulties or to being single. I see you. God sees you." It resonated with me. It tugged at a desire deep within my heart that I had been suppressing — the desire to be a mother.

Do you long for children? Do you desire to be a mother? Singleness can be difficult because we see it as hindering us from being who we want to be and in fulfilling innate desires of motherhood. And there's nothing we can do to control or change it.

I would love to have a son one day to name Hugh after my brother, father, grandfather, and great-grandfather. I would raise him to fear God and serve Him wholeheartedly just like they did and are doing. I also desire a little girl to teach how to love others well and how to host great parties where people from all seasons of life can come and find that they belong.

Is this to be written in my story? Only God knows. It isn't at this moment, so I must trust His timing and remain joyful. I have other single friends who have the same intense desires. I also have married friends who struggle with infertility. And then there are the mothers who have children who have walked out, leaving them feeling childless again. Sometimes we have these good and godly desires that God hasn't allowed to play out at this time.

I was listening to Beth Moore teach on James recently and was encouraged by a profound thought: I *can* be a mother right now — in the faith. I can mother spiritual children.[4]

Paul was single, yet he fathered two spiritual sons — Titus and Timothy. "To Titus, my *true son* in our common faith" (Titus 1:4 HCSB, emphasis added). "To Timothy my *true son* in the faith" (I Timothy 1:2 HCSB, emphasis added). Paul himself was spiritually mothered by a faithful woman. At the end of his letter to the Romans, he instructs the saints in Rome to "Greet Rufus, chosen in the Lord; also his mother, *who has been a mother to me as well*" (Romans 16:13 ESV, Emphasis added).

Jesus is another example of spiritual parenting. Eugene Peterson says, Jesus "himself did not procreate children, yet by his love he made us all sons and daughters (Mt

12:46-50) . . . Among those around us we develop sons and daughters, sisters and brothers even as our Lord did with us: 'Oh, how blessed are you parents with your quivers full of children!'"[5]

How many *true sons* and *daughters* in the faith do you have? How full is your quiver? You never know the spiritual impact you may have on the next generation. This season can be one of praying for children in the faith to shepherd into becoming men and women of God. Maybe this looks like teaching a four- and five-year-old class at church on Sundays, going to coffee with that teen girl each week, or opening your home during the week to host a small group.

Just because I am not a physical mom who is celebrated and remembered on Mother's Day this year does not mean that I cannot be a spiritual mom. I can love those around me. I can nurture new believers. I can encourage the girls in my small group. I can teach my students at school. I can volunteer for the church nursery. I can mentor that high school girl.

Know that the desire to be a mother is God-given. But for today, embrace the opportunities to live out that desire as God has allowed in this season — by mothering children in the faith. God sees you. He knows. Lift up your hands in praise to the God Who creates good out of nothing.

Tired of Waiting

Singleness equals waiting. This is often the thought that comes to mind when women find themselves in this season. But guess what? Working equals waiting. Marriage equals waiting. Being a parent equals waiting.

You will never stop waiting for something.

My married friend is waiting for a baby. My father is waiting for retirement. My coworker is waiting for restoration in her marriage. My neighbor is waiting for a new job. Don't think you are alone in the waiting. Don't think that once your longing in this season ends you will be done waiting forever.

Earthly waiting reveals a spiritual waiting that God has placed within the believing heart. As believers, we are waiting on greater things than we could imagine. We are waiting on Jesus to make everything right and to claim His Bride, the Church. Courtney Doctor, in an article for Together For the Gospel, reminds us, "If you're waiting on something, remember that, ultimately, it's the Lord you're waiting on."[6] These earthly waitings make known the pains for heavenly longings.

So take comfort in the waiting of this season, and let it remind you that your heart is truly yearning for all to be settled by Jesus. Isaiah 40:31 says, "but they who wait for the LORD shall renew their strength; they shall mount up with wings like eagles; they shall run and not be weary; they shall walk and not faint" (ESV).

Miracles in the Unknown

In the Armor of God study, Priscilla Shirer says, "Sometimes the greatest miracles God does are not in our circumstances, it's in our minds."[7] A single woman wanting to be dating, a dating woman wanting to be engaged, an engaged woman wanting to be married, a married woman wanting to be pregnant . . . will we ever be content? The wanting is not wrong. Those desires are natural and God-given. We pray and ask God for the next season and for Him to work. Perhaps, though, we miss the fact that God *is* at work. He is working right now in *this* season, whatever season that may be.

A great miracle may be found in God's answering your prayers for a godly man, but the greatest miracle may be found in surrendering and being content where you are. Only then can you fully enjoy the miracles to come.

Learn to Laugh

With all of the unknowns ahead, it's time to laugh with joyful expectancy for what God may bring into your life. Proverbs 31:25 says of a virtuous woman, "She is clothed with strength and dignity, and she laughs without fear of the future" (NLT). How can we embrace the unknowns ahead? By clothing ourselves with strength and dignity and learning to laugh.

Strength is "the capacity of an object or substance to withstand great force or pressure."[8] Tomorrow will bring great force and pressures into your life. Will you be able to withstand? Lean into Jesus Who withstood Satan's temptations and the brutality of the cross.

Dignity is defined as "the quality of being worthy of honor or respect."[9] We gain that dignity by opening our Bibles and mirroring the One worthy of all honor and respect.

When life is filled with the unexpected, you cling to the Expected. When life is unsure, you cling to the Sure. When people leave you, you cling to the One Who stays. You must know the Expected, or the unexpected will shatter you. You must know Sure, or the unsure will leave you questioning and wondering. You must know the One Who stays, or you will be left behind when those people leave. Know Jesus. Spend time with Him. He is the Expected, the Sure, the One Who never leaves.

With unknowns ahead, it's time to build strength and dignity into our lives. Then go ahead. It's okay - throw back your head and laugh at the year to come "for the joy of the Lord is your strength."[10]

SCENE 11

The Author

The Author. The Script Writer of our lives. God dips His pen into the ink of love and heavenly purpose and authors a beautiful story of redemption for each of His daughters.

In the midst of our chapters of singleness, we can find ourselves tempted with several different responses to the One with the pen. We can totally forget about God. We can get so caught up in finding the perfect man that we miss out on the truly perfect Man. Or we can bitterly blame God as being the cause for our singleness and a hindrance to getting what we want. We label Him as unkind and uncaring. If God cared, then why didn't He just write a godly man into my story? We also try to bribe God in order to get what we want. We try to manipulate Him by using things dear to His heart - prayer, good works, serving, reading His Word. It works with people — why wouldn't it work with God?

What you think about God, the Author of your story and the Lover of your soul, is the most important thing about you.[1] How you view Him and if you take Him at His Word shows where your faith and trust is. Look for the loving God behind the pen. Learn the heart of the Script Writer. What He writes (or doesn't write) into your life is meant to point you back to Him.

The Author Gives You Purpose

Let's talk about goals and purpose because if you think that your sole purpose on earth is to get married and be happy, then you will be sorely disappointed. Marriage is not the goal, and happiness is not the goal. The goal is to look more like Jesus. You will not arrive when you get married. Marriage can be a dream and a longing, but if you put all your expectations and hopes into this covenant, you will be let down. If you do end up getting married, you will be transferring those hopes onto your husband and putting pressure on him to meet unrealistic expectations.

The only covenant you can depend on is the one between God and His Bride, the Church. He sent His Son to die for the sins of the world so that we might be reconciled to Him. Our purpose is to be restored to Him, to know Him, and to glorify Him. God can use singleness or marriage to accomplish His plans. Know that an earthly relationship status, while it may be a means for the greater goal that God has for you, is not the end purpose for your life.

If you put all of your hopes in marriage, you will be dissatisfied. You will be disheartened if you *do not* get married, and you will be disappointed if you *do* get married because marriage is not the end-all-be-all. Pursuing Jesus is.

The Author Has Given You the Perfect Man

The years of singleness that God scripted for me have taught me that no earthly man can fulfill my heart's longing. I have tasted the goodness of the perfect Man, Jesus Christ. I have learned more of His ways during times when there is no one else to whom I can turn. He has been the only Man Who is always there for me during the ups and downs of my singleness journey. When I didn't know what that guy at church thought of me, I could find God's exact thoughts toward me in His Word. When I was ghosted, I knew that Jesus was still with me. He never leaves me nor forsakes me. Jesus shows me ultimate love. He forgives my every wrongdoing. He romances my heart and whispers tender words of faithful love. He knows me better than even I know myself. He is patient, kind, trustworthy, attentive, selfless.

If the Lord writes marriage into my script one day, I truly believe my husband will thank God for my years of singleness. I look back at my twenty-one-year-old self and think of how much expectation I would have put on my husband to fulfill my desires and to be everything that only Jesus could be for me. I know those struggles to place expectations on someone else will never fully go away, but I have tasted the sweet affection of Jesus and learned the beauty of depending on Him. I pray my heart will have the habit of remaining there. My mind knows that I will be let down by the people in my life but also that I can always trust the love of my Father. In your search for the "perfect man," know that you will never find him here on earth; rather, you can find Him in Heaven and on the pages of Scripture. When you put all of your expectations and your hope in Jesus, you will not be disappointed.

The Author's Character

It is so easy to look at our lives and magnify what God is *not* doing, what God has *not* given us, the pain He *has* allowed. We point fingers at God and think of Him as unkind, unloving, unfair. As previously mentioned, God's character should not be interpreted in light of our circumstances; rather, our circumstances should be interpreted in light of His character.

When we experience pain and unfulfilled desires, Scripture should be where we land first. We ought to filter our thoughts, emotions, and beliefs through the Word of God. We should pause and say, "Wait, this *seems* unkind of God. But I *know* and *believe* that He is kind. Lord, help me see your kindness in this." We can also confess, "God! I see no good in this pain, but I *know* You say You are good. Give me eyes to see Your goodness." We can choose to interpret our circumstances based on the trustworthy character of the Author.

Let me encourage you to keep going even though it is not easy. I call it "a holy struggle."

As I mentioned previously, we *know* God is kind. We *believe* God is good. But then we experience life around us. We see the hurt and the injustice. Hurt and misunderstandings could lead us to reject what God says is true, to walk away from Him, or to be apathetic and not care to struggle at all. The holy response is to struggle *toward* God, not *away from* God. The struggle is holy because we believe, and we want the understanding to accompany the belief. We see our situation. We see the truth of Who God is, and we do not know what to do with the gap between the two. So we can pray and ask God to fill in the gap between the circumstances and who we believe Him to be with supernatural faith and confidence from the Spirit. We echo the father of the demon-possessed son in Mark 9:24, "I do believe! Help my unbelief" (HCSB).

When life and faith get confusing — and they will — fall on your knees with your holy struggle and humbly proclaim to the Lord, "I believe! Help my unbelief."

Using the Author

We can, more often than we care to admit, view God as someone to manipulate. We think of Him as a genie, only called upon to get our wish fulfilled. Are you seeking God only to get what you want? Are you using Him as a means to an end? If so, you are missing out. Jesus is all in all. Spending time with God and serving Him are not meant to be used as ways to get Him to give you a husband, the perfect image, directions for the next steps in your life, or whatever it is that you desire. A.W. Tozer said that "Whoever seeks God as a means toward desired ends will not find God. The mighty God, the maker of heaven and earth, will not be one of the many treasures, not even the chief of all treasures. He will be all in all or He will be nothing."[2] As mentioned previously in Scenes 3 and 8, the Christian walk is not a formula. God is not a means to an end. He is not a vending machine God where you put in money and get what you want out of Him. He desires a relationship. Seek God to know God. He is to be our highly prized treasure. Do not try to use Him; instead, get to know Him.

Talking to the Author in Prayer

The lifeline of the single life — of any aspect of life — is prayer. It is the way to talk to and listen to the Author. It's our communication. Prayer is beautiful and mysterious.

Asking

In Matthew, Jesus tells His followers to,

Keep asking, and it will be given to you. Keep searching, and you will find. Keep knocking, and the door will be opened to you. For everyone who asks receives, and the one who searches finds, and to the one who knocks, the door will be opened. What man among you, if his son asks him for bread, will give him a stone? Or if he asks for a fish, will give him a snake? If you then, who are evil, know how to give good gifts to your children, how much more will your Father in heaven give good things to those who ask Him! (Matthew 7:7-11 HCSB).

For a few years during my single journey, I was scared to pray and ask for a husband. I feared that my desire was bad because it was not being immediately answered. But the truth is that we all have unfulfilled desires — we wanted the job we interviewed for, we wished for different family dynamics, we wanted to look like her, etc. My desire has always been for a godly husband. I had prayed for years, but God had not delivered yet, so I stopped asking.

While I do not understand prayer and asking and how it all works, I do know that our prayers make a difference. I know that God says that sometimes we do not have because we do not ask. So I can pray and keep asking. I want to be like the persistent widow who keeps seeking because she knows the One to Whom she prays can deliver. Do not ever be afraid to boldly approach the throne and bring your requests to a God who cares about your desires. He knows the desires of my heart but longs for me to bring them to Him.

However, just because you ask does not mean that you will receive exactly that which you request. When I look back on my prayers from the past, I thank God that He wisely did not give me all that I asked for. But also know that, as the Matthew passage above says, your Father is not a stone-giving Father or a snake-giving Father. He is the One Who gives above and beyond what we could ever imagine He could give.[3]

Praying for Your Singleness

What if you started praying just as intentionally over your season of singleness as you do for a future husband or for a future endeavor? Fear can keep us from praying. We wonder, "What if God actually answers my prayers and starts to use my singleness? I'm not sure I want Him to do that. I'd rather He use me in marriage or in another job position or where I feel comfortable." You are missing out on what God could be doing through you right now! We long for the future, the next thing; but once that comes, we neglect to water it with the same intensity of intercession. It is good and natural to pray for the future, but don't forget to pray over what God is doing today, in this season.

A few summers ago, I was challenged by a missionary friend to start praying over different areas of my life. Singleness was an area that I struggled with but wanted God to use. It felt like a 'meh' area of my life, and I longed for it to be a thriving tool for His Kingdom.

So I started to pray. Everyday. "Lord, as an unmarried woman, help me to be concerned about the things of the Lord, about your things, not mine. I want to be holy in my body and in my spirit so I can better serve you. I don't know how long this season will last, but I know I want it to be used for your glory. Do your work."

And God started moving. He started answering.

He led me to start a small group for other single women. He led me to create a blog on singleness. He led me to start a social media platform where single women can be encouraged, challenged, and loved. Then He led me to write this book. He is still on the move, and I can't wait to see where He leads next.

God's plan for your season of singleness will not look the same as His plan for mine. It may look like serving in the preschool ministry each Sunday. It may involve discipling high school girls. It may be starting a widow's ministry at your church. It will be unique to you and your gifting. The Church needs your season of singleness. God longs for your season to be used for Him. Start being intentional about praying boldly over your singleness. Then just watch what He will do.

Praising

Do you ever have reality checks? Maybe you find yourself thinking, "Oh my goodness! I'm thirty, and my life does not look like I thought it would." Or perhaps your thoughts look more like, "I was just sitting here getting my hair cut ten weeks ago, and she is asking me what's new in my life and I have nothing." Usually this happens for me on birthdays or when I show up to the family Thanksgiving again, and I feel the same as last year and the year before. Maybe it's Valentine's Day or Christmas for you.

We consider these to be life's milestones. A milestone is "a stone functioning as a milepost; a significant event or stage in the life, progress, development, or the like of a person."[4] We all have these mental checkpoints where we want to do "this" by the time we are "this many" years old. *I want to be married by the time I'm thirty. I want to have my dream career by the time I'm thirty-five. I want to have children after three years of marriage. I'd like to be engaged by the spring so I can plan a fall wedding.* We set up these milestones or checkups to keep us on track to accomplish our desires and goals.

Then life.

Life isn't Instagram perfect. We wake up on Valentine's Day, only to be reminded that we had hoped last year that this year would be different. Thirty rolls around, and you have no men in your life in whom you would even be interested. The dream career proves to be financially impossible at this stage. And he surely doesn't seem to be popping the question anytime soon.

What do you do at those milestones?

Set up an Ebenezer.

"Afterward, Samuel took a stone and set it upright between Mizpah and Shen. He named it Ebenezer, explaining, 'The LORD has helped us to this point'" (I Samuel 7:12 HCSB). God helped the Israelites defeat the Philistines; and Samuel, in an act of worship, set up a commemoration of this event. Ebenezer means "a stone of help; a commemoration of divine assistance."[5] Samuel saw the battle; he saw the victory and raised a hallelujah. He set up a stone and proclaimed, "We are here because of God. The Lord has helped us to this point."

The same is true for you. The Lord has helped you to this point. What will you do with these milestones of life?

> *See the battle that has been waged over your soul.* The enemy whispers the lies of not good enough, lonely, never going to happen, unloved, forgotten.

> *See the victory.* God's Word says Christ is enough for you. He will never leave you. He knows the desires of your heart and withholds no good thing from you.

You are loved. God thought of you before the foundation of the world.

Set up your Ebenezer. See that God has brought you to today, to this milestone. He has helped you make it to this point in the journey. He has worked all things for your good.

So when you come upon a milestone, set up your Ebenezer and raise your hallelujah.

The Author and the Planner

"I don't know the plan, but I *do* know the Planner!" My uncle David said this last year when he found out that he was diagnosed with Chronic Lymphocytic Leukemia (a cancer of the blood and bone marrow). It has spoken to me deeply, and I have found myself meditating on it.

I am a big-time planner, and I like to know the plan. But God doesn't always let me in on His ways. He simply asks me to trust. I know His "goodness and faithful love will pursue me all the days of my life" (Psalm 23:6 CSB). What does that look like? I'm not sure, for God tells me that "for as the heavens are higher than the earth, so are my ways higher than your ways and my thoughts than your thoughts" (Isaiah 55:9 ESV). My definitions of love and goodness are not the same as His.

It's easy to trust when we think we know the plan or when things are going according to the way we would like. But I am so encouraged and challenged when I see people like my uncle, like my single friends, like *you*, trusting even when the plan is unknown and unsure. We do not know all that our scripts hold; it feels like we are playing impromptu parts. However, we *do* know the kindness of the Script Writer. And we can trust the surety of His un-changeableness.

I encourage you, friend, as I encourage myself — trust God. He is the Giver of all good things. Ask for your desires. Pray boldly that God will use this season. Set up Ebenezers that remind you of His goodness. Trust that the Author planned your script before time began. Then step into your role and boldly live out the life to which He has lovingly called you.

SCENE 12

The Final Act

Growing up, I loved to act. I just knew that I was destined to be a movie star. My imagination was wild and vivid, and I would often write and star in my own plays. In my childhood home, we had a brick fireplace and hearth, big enough to be used as a stage. So I would create tickets, charge admission, and welcome family and church friends into the audience to cheer me on.

The first time I ever auditioned for a role in a real play was in fifth grade. My family had just moved to a new state, and we started attending a new church. I knew no one. But the perfect way to make my debut in this new life was, in my mind, to be the star in the church Christmas production. I had great confidence since my acting career had already started off so well.

I auditioned for the lead role . . . and landed the role of an oriental pot. No joke. They painted a piece of cardboard and cut a hole for my face to poke through. I was mortified. To make matters worse, a third grader ended up with the lead role. I was so embarrassed that when my parents dropped me off for practice each week, I would run and hide in the church. I ended up getting in trouble for skipping because apparently I needed to be there for all ten practices so I knew exactly where to enter with my head poking through the vase and when to exit. Bless my fifth grade heart.

Being an oriental pot in fifth grade was mortifying for sure. Now, looking back, I have a good laugh and a good story to tell.

But sometimes I can relate to that oriental pot role I played. My season of singleness can feel mortifying and unwanted; I can find myself wanting to run and hide, skipping out on what life currently offers me. Of course, the analogy breaks down because God has not written the role of an oriental pot for me. He sent His Son Jesus to die on the cross and resurrect three days later so I could play out the role of a daughter of the King, cherished and loved.

My hope and prayer for you is that you will not find yourself embarrassed and hiding during this season of singleness — however long or short it may be. I pray God will transform your heart and mind to see the beauty that has been written. You are not a stagehand or an extra. You are playing the leading lady in your life with the goal of reflecting the goodness and kindness of God to the audience.

So step into the spotlight and shine brightly for the glory of the Script Writer because your life has been *Beautifully Scripted*.

Notes

ACT I: *The Leading Actress*

SCENE 1: **Understanding My Character**

1. Wilkin, Jen. *Women of the Word: How to Study the Bible with Both Our Hearts and Our Minds.* 1st ed. Wheaton, IL: Crossway, 2014.

2. Scutti, Susan. "Loneliness Peaks at Three Key Ages, Study Finds." CNN. Cable News Network, December 20, 2018. https://www-m.cnn.com/2018/12/18/health/loneliness-peaks-study/index.html.

3. Elliot, Elisabeth. *Let Me Be a Woman.* Carol Stream, IL: Tyndale Momentum, 1999.

4. Bonikowsky, Andy. *The Aierdi Miracle.* Mauldin, SC: CTS Publications, 2013.

SCENE 2: **The Mind**

1. Holmes, Phillip. "The Evangelical Drug of Choice." Desiring God, July 20, 2016. https://www.desiringgod.org/articles/the-evangelical-drug-of-choice.

2. Tripp, Paul David. "Talking to Yourself." Paul Tripp, March 13, 2013. https://www.paultripp.com/wednesdays-word/posts/talking-to-yourself.

SCENE 3: **What Did I Do Wrong?**

1. Prosperity Gospel: "The so-called prosperity gospel is a perversion of the biblical gospel, according to

which Jesus is a means to the blessings of health, wealth, and power. The preachers of this 'gospel' may quote God's word, but twist it to support their false theology." Tamfu, Dieudonné. "The Gods of the Prosperity Gospel: Unmasking American Idols in Africa." Desiring God, February 4, 2020. https://www.desiringgod.org/articles/the-gods-of-the-prosperity-gospel.

2. TerKeurst, Lysa. *Trustworthy*. Nashville, TN: Lifeway, 2019.

3. Piper, John. "Job: When the Righteous Suffer, Part 1." Desiring God, October 17, 2008. https://www.desiringgod.org/messages/job-when-the-righteous-suffer-part-1.

SCENE 4: **Living the Life**

1. Wilkin, Jen. *Women of the Word: How to Study the Bible with Both Our Hearts and Our Minds*. 1st ed. Wheaton, IL: Crossway, 2014.

2. Allberry, Sam. *7 Myths about Singleness*. Wheaton, IL: Crossway, 2019.

3. Information on Dave Ramsey's Financial Peace University can be found on his website: https://www.daveramsey.com.

SCENE 5: **The Tragedy of Heartbreak**

1. Borgueta, Maya. "The Psychology of Ghosting: Why People Do It and a Better Way to Break Up." HuffPost. HuffPost, December 6, 2017. https://

www.huffpost.com/entry/the-psychology-of-ghostin_b_7999858.

ACT II: *The Supporting Actors*

SCENE 6: **Dating**

1. Warman, Kait, and Jamal Miller. "Heart of Dating." *Heart of Dating*, May 8, 2019. https://heartofdating.com/047-how-to-become-the-one-with-the-7-steps-to-prepare-for-marriage-with-jamal-miller/.

2. Piper, John. "Ask Pastor John." *Ask Pastor John*. Desiring God, August 12, 2014. https://www.desiringgod.org/interviews/is-online-dating-good-for-christians.

3. Lewis, C. S. *The Four Loves*. Boston, MA: Harvest Books, 1971.

4. Note: Pastor Nick did not originate this thought. This quote came as a result of his reading multiple sources. I could not locate the original quotes.

5. This was my version of a quote by Thabiti Anyabwile: "As women grow older, the sense that it might not happen for them grows increasingly strong. Baucham reckons that age 14, young girls are looking for 'the total package' and are unwilling to settle. By age 24, their list is wittled down to 'a good godly man.' And by age 34 they're happy if 'the man knows where a church is.'" Anyabwile, Thabiti. "What a Husband Must Be." Together For the Gospel, August 19, 2008. https://

www.thegospelcoalition.org/blogs/thabiti-any-abwile/what-husband-must-be/.

6. Segal, Marshall. "When the Not-Yet Married Meet." Desiring God, June 6, 2013. https://www.desiringgod.org/articles/when-the-not-yet-married-meet.

7. The term sexual integrity is used often by Dr. Juli Slattery in *Rethinking Sexuality*. "When applied to sexuality, integrity means that everything we believe about sexuality is completely consistent with how we live." Slattery, Juli. *Rethinking Sexuality*. Colorado Springs, CO: Multnomah, 2018.

8. Slattery, Juli. *Rethinking Sexuality*. Colorado Springs, CO: Multnomah, 2018.

9. Moore, Beth. *James: Mercy Triumphs*. Nashville, TN: LifeWay, 2011.

10. See John 8:11.

11. Moore, Beth. *James: Mercy Triumphs*. Nashville, TN: LifeWay, 2011.

12. Warman, Kait, and Jamal Miller. "Heart of Dating." *Heart of Dating*, May 8, 2019. https://heartofdating.com/047-how-to-become-the-one-with-the-7-steps-to-prepare-for-marriage-with-jamal-miller/.

SCENE 7: **When Her Script Is What I Want**

1. Downs, Annie F. "Two Lost Sons." YouTube. CrossPoint, February 19, 2019. https://www.youtube.com/watch?v=43EtdzOUsf8.

2. C.J. Mahaney Quote found in *Boy Meets Girl*. Harris, Joshua, and C. J. Mahaney. *Boy Meets Girl*. Sisters, OR: Multnomah, 2000.

SCENE 8: **She Spoke into My Script**

1. See I Corinthians 13:4-7.

2. Jenilyn Swett quoted in Christianity Today article. Courtney Ellis. "How Single Women Help New Moms Make It Through." Christianity Today, February 2019. https://www.christianitytoday.com/women/2019/april/singleness-motherhood-single-women-help-new-moms-make-it.html.

SCENE 9: **The Troupe**

1. See Ephesians 4:11-16.

2. See Hebrews 10:24.

3. See Matthew 18:20, Galatians 6:2, Proverbs 27:17, James 5:16, 2 Timothy 3:16-17, and Hebrews 3:13.

4. "Hospitality." Dictionary. Dictionary.com. Accessed May 31, 2020. https://www.dictionary.com/browse/hospitality?s=t.

ACT III: The Author

SCENE 10: **Unknown Endings**

1. "Even If." *Genius,* February 17, 2017, genius.com/Mercyme-even-if-lyrics.

2. *Romans.* Scotland, UK: Marshall Pickering, 1999, 207.

3. *Romans.* Scotland, UK: Marshall Pickering, 1999, 207.

4. Moore, Beth. *James: Mercy Triumphs.* Nashville, TN: LifeWay, 2011.

5. Peterson, Eugene H. *A Long Obedience in the Same Direction.* Downers Grove, IL: InterVarsity Press, 2019.

6. Doctor, Courtney. "Hope for Waiting Hearts." The Gospel Coalition, January 26, 2018. https://www.thegospelcoalition.org/article/hope-for-waiting-hearts/.

7. Shirer, Priscilla. *The Armor of God.* Nashville, TN: Lifeway, 2015.

8. "Strength: Definition of Strength by Lexico." Lexico Dictionaries | English. Lexico Dictionaries. Accessed June 1, 2020. https://www.lexico.com/en/definition/strength.

9. "Dignity: Definition of Dignity by Lexico." Lexico Dictionaries | English. Lexico Dictionaries. Accessed June 1, 2020. https://www.lexico.com/en/definition/dignity.

10. See Nehemiah 8:10b.

SCENE 11: **The Author**

1. "What comes into our minds when we think about God is the most important thing about us . . . Worship is pure or base as the worshiper entertains high or low thoughts of God."

Tozer, A. W. *The Knowledge of the Holy.* San Francisco, CA: HarperOne, 2009.

2. Tozer, A. W., Wiersbe, Warren W. *The Best of A.W. Tozer.* Camp Hill, PA: WingSpread Publishers, 2007.

3. See Ephesians 3:20.

4. "Milestone." Dictionary. Dictionary.com. Accessed June 1, 2020. https://www.dictionary.com/browse/milestone.

5. "Ebenezer." Dictionary. Dictionary.com. Accessed June 1, 2020. https://www.dictionary.com/browse/ebenezer?s=t. "Ebenezer." Merriam-Webster. Accessed June 1, 2020. https://www.merriam-webster.com/dictionary/ebenezer.

About Lauren McCoy

Lauren is passionate about Jesus and loves walking alongside other women in their faith journeys. She is a fan of small groups and studying the Bible together. Lauren spends her working hours as an English as a Second Language teacher at a large high school outside of Nashville, Tennessee. Otherwise, you can probably find her drinking coffee at a local coffee shop with friends or enjoying physical activity such as indoor rock climbing, spin class, or hiking.

Lauren would love to connect with you! You can find her here:

Facebook: www.facebook.com/singledoutforhim/
Instagram: singledoutforhim
Blog: www.singledoutforhim.co

Share what you are learning and reading! Tag @singledoutforhim on social media and use the following hashtags: #beautifullyscripted and #singledoutforhim

Curtain Call

In a play, the curtain call is where all the actors and actresses come out after the show is over to take a bow. For *Beautifully Scripted,* there were many involved who helped this book become a reality. Many of them would like to stay behind the scenes, but I want to call them to the stage and clap for the part they played in this book.

Mom, Dad, Austen, Julie: Thank you for believing in me, praying for me, and cheering me on each step of the way. I have appreciated all the feedback in our Fam Bam text group along the way. Haven and Sydney: Thank you for bringing me joy and providing much-needed fun breaks as I wrote this book.

Susan: How can I ever thank you enough for all that you have done? You have spent countless hours reading, rereading, editing, eating a splice of comma cake (better than grandma!), talking on the phone, and encouraging me along the way. Thanks for the laughter and for helping me stay sane.

Lawren: Singled Out for Him would not be the blog or website that it is today without your knowledge and expertise. You have spent many hours helping me and giving advice. Thanks for praying for me, being excited at God's work, and encouraging me every step of the way.

My editing team: Kristen, Katherine, Elizabeth, Julie, Jessica, Lawren, Grace, Shea, Joanie, and Emily. Thank you for being a part of the launch team. I valued your input and loved reading your comments and encouragement along the way. Thanks for helping me realize the difference between a – and a — .

Susanne: Thank you for mentoring me and praying for me. God has greatly used you in my life.

Jill: Thanks for believing my dream (way back in high school) of writing a book. You were always my biggest cheerleader! And now — ten years later, it is a reality.

To so many people along the way: God has greatly used you in my singleness journey. I am forever grateful for the prayers, check-ins, conversations, and encouragement.

CUE: APPLAUSE!

Made in the USA
Monee, IL
06 March 2021